THE BOATBUILDERS
of Muskoka

Ditchburn's Shop c 1905 (left to right) Herb Ditchburn, Alf Ditchburn (sitting), unknown, Ernie Greavette and Tom Greavette.

THE BOATBUILDERS
of Muskoka

A.H. DUKE and W.M. GRAY

A BOSTON MILLS PRESS BOOK

Duke, A.H. (Audrey Harold), 1908 -
    The boatbuilders of Muskoka

ISBN 1-55046-0749

1. Boatyards - Ontario - Muskoka (District municipality) -
History. 2. Launch industry - Ontario - Muskoka
(District municipality) - History.
I. Gray, W.M. (William Melville), 1953 -
II. Title.

VM321.52.C3D95 1985   338.7'6238231   C85-099304-0

Published in 1992 by
Stoddart Publishing Co. Limited
34 Lesmill Road
Toronto, Canada
M3B 2T6

A BOSTON MILLS PRESS BOOK
The Boston Mills Press
132 Main St.
Erin, Ontario
N0B 1T0

Winners of the
Heritage Canada
Communications Award

American Association
for State and Local History
Award Winner

The publisher gratefully acknowledges the support of The Canada Council, Ontario Arts Council and Ontario Publishing Centre in the development of writing and publishing in Canada.

Printed and bound in Canada by John Deyell Company

CONTENTS

- DEDICATION -

This work is respectfully dedicated to the hundreds of men; the craftsmen and mechanics of the district who, over the decades, built some of the finest launches to be found on North American waters. The business acumen, skill and artistry of Ditchburn, Minett, Greavette, Shields, and the other known names of the industry would have counted for little if not backed up by that great pool of the unsung and unnamed. The families of these men can look back with pride on their contribution to this unique and special aspect of our Muskokan and Canadian heritage.

FOREWORD

For many years I felt strongly that the story should be told of the builders and craftsmen who produced the incomparable pleasure launches of Muskoka; so when Georgian College asked me to speak on this subject for their Heritage Muskoka series in 1977, I readily agreed. My illustrated talk proved very popular with boating enthusiasts, who encouraged me to put the material and pictures into book form.

Last year when Bill Gray offered to assist me on my project, he provided the needed impetus. He has been very helpful in gathering further information and putting the book together, and I guess I would not have even got started on this project if it had not been for my wife Dorothy prodding me from the outset. To them both I owe a lot of credit.

In all trades there are good and bad, but most boat builders are basically dedicated souls. A good many started in the craft after public school and continued throughout their working life. Unfortunately, boat building was always a poorly-paid job. A carpenter could go out with little more than hammer and saw to build a house and do better financially. The reason for this seeming disparity is that at the end of the day the carpenter had something to show for his work, while the boat builder quite often struggled on all day in a bushel basket.

The Muskoka Lakes-type boat was not a boat you could build with production line facilities; most wooden boats are one of a kind — like a Turkish rug — there are no two exactly the same.

This book is not intended to be the definitive history of boat building in Muskoka. We have attempted here to present a relatively comprehensive survey of the major builders of pleasure boats on the three Muskoka lakes. There were several other men who built the odd motor boat over the winter, but boat building was not their livelihood and we have not included them. A number of others built commercial boats; steamers, tugs, scows, rowboats and canoes, and they too fall outside the scope of this work.

We have made every effort to be accurate but as virtually no records for most of the businesses have survived, a great deal of our information is based on memories — often second hand — of events that took place long ago.

Without the cooperation and help of a great number of people who shared their knowledge of this special aspect of our past — and more tangibly their photographs — this work would have been almost impossible to tackle. Its success can be attributed directly to them.

Shortcomings, the gaps and inadvert errors we trust will be met with understanding.

INTRODUCTION

We have attempted here to outline something of the stories of the different pleasure-boat builders of Muskoka. It is virtually impossible today to write the definitive account — we are twenty five years too late to get even a relatively comprehensive account. Practically all of the people have passed on; the old firms are long gone and their records dispersed.

The Great Depression tried the industry sorely and the trend to fibreglass and inboard outboards from the 1950s very nearly administered the coup de grâce.

This past decade has witnessed a minor renaissance, however, as the interest shown in the classic hand-crafted wooden launch of those palmy days between the wars has been renewed.

The 'Muskoka Boat' to Muskokans is a genre unto itself, and none here will dispute the claim that the standards of artistry, woodworking and finishing were unsurpassed elsewhere. There is, admittedly, a certain satisfaction and smug comfort in such parochialism, but there is ample evidence left on these lakes today to bear out the claim.

Muskoka waters lend themselves to boating. The three large interconnected lakes with their mile upon mile of broken shoreline, studded with innumerable islands, offer a marvellous scenic and extensive — yet protected — opportunity for weeks of cruising.

At the same time that Muskoka was opened to settlement in the 1860s it was discovered by tourists. Resort development paralleled the establishment of permanent settlements, and the local economy became increasingly dependent upon tourism as the century drew to a close. Through the 1880s and 1890s Muskoka became known as a 'place of resort and fashion', as an

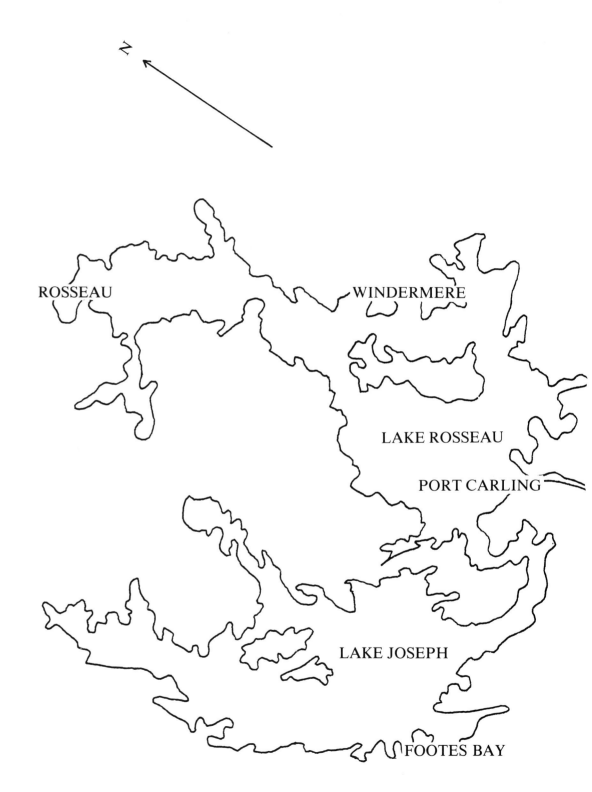

ROSSEAU

WINDERMERE

LAKE ROSSEAU

PORT CARLING

LAKE JOSEPH

FOOTES BAY

BRACEBRIDGE

BEAUMARIS

LAKE MUSKOKA

GRAVENHURST

BALA

1. (left to right) Kay Moyes (Duke), Aud Duke, Len Amey, Claude Duke, Lorraine Amey (Cope), Alva Wilson (Duke) in a rowboat built c. 1875.

ever-increasing number of leading families from Pittsburg, Buffalo, Cleveland, Hamilton and Toronto made an annual trek to the Highlands of Ontario a part of their yearly itinerary.

The rocky terrain, swamps and hard winters did not encourage land transport, and economic necessity dictated the establishment of all the major population centres on the navigable waters to be served by the admirable A.P. Cockburn's line of steamers. A demand for boats became immediately apparent and a number of men turned their hands to building work boats; scows, steam tugs, supply boats as well as the big steamers of the Muskoka Lakes Navigation Company. In addition, a good number of dugouts, and later rowboats and canoes were built, first for personal transportation and then to rent out to the ever-increasing number of tourists who stayed at the summer boarding houses and hotels.

Henry Ditchburn of Rosseau and William Johnston of Port Carling soon became the proprietors of large boat liveries with branches all around the lakes.

Gasoline-powered motorboats made their appearance on the Lakes in the early 1890s but these early boats were paddled and rowed far more than they proceeded under their own power. It was not until the early years of this century that these lakes — for so many years domain of the reciprocating steam engine — became home of a significant number of motor boats. The two most successful boat builders, Ditchburn and Johnston, pioneered the domestic building of gasoline motorboats.

The pool of skilled boatbuilders living on these waters, in conjunction with the great concentration of wealth among the summer residents from both sides of the border, fostered a local custom boat building industry. From the turn of the century to the Second World War, Muskoka was the centre of some of the finest work done on the continent.

Gasoline motorboats to begin with were simply steam launches with different power plants. Usually between 18 and 30 feet in length, they were built of cedar, cyprus (or occasionally pine), with oak or elm ribs, stems and decks; they were heavy, sturdy and eminently serviceable. As a rule they were built with one large cockpit lined with benches, the engine exposed and mounted mid-ships. They were invariably painted white with a green or red bottom. The primitive engines were very large, heavy and slow-turning — by even the standards of the 1920s — compared to the power they turned out. More important, they were undependable and demanded constant attention.

In the first few years of this century a number of people in Toronto started to build gasoline engines specifically for marine use, in one, two and three-cylinder models. One of these manufacturers was imaginatively named 'The Gasoline Engine Co.'.

Remarkable technological advances were made in the development of the gasoline marine engine in a very few years and, with the resultant increase in reliability and power, the market exploded, warranting the organization of an industry based on the production of launches.

The pioneers of the industry in Muskoka were Henry Ditchburn, William Johnston and Hubert Minett. Before the First War the most significant of these three was the operation of Henry and his nephew Herb Ditchburn — the H. Ditchburn Pleasure Boat Co. Ltd. Before we take a look at the various boat building enterprises, we will take a brief survey of the actual mechanics of building a launch illustrated with views from Ditchburn's operations in 1920 and examine the different types of launches that were built.

2, 3, 4, Typical launches photographed in the vicinity of Port Sandfield, 1907.

5. An early gasoline engine. A 4 cylinder standard from 1905.

BOATBUILDING

When a builder undertakes to build a boat, he has to know what type of boat is required; how long she is to be, how wide (beam), whether she is to be round bilge, smoothskin or lapstrake, or Vee bottom. Will she be forward drive (engine aft of the main cockpit and driven from the front seat) or centre-drive (main cockpit behind the engine and driven from aft of the engine)?.

With any design, the Stock is the first thing to be set up. This is a plank on its edge, cut to fit the shape the keel is to be. This plank is held about 24 inches off the floor with angular supports about every 3 or 4 feet apart. (see photo number 1)

The Keel is the backbone of the boat and after having the Bow Stem attached, is fastened down on to the Stock with a few screws which will be removed and the holes plugged after the hull is built. The Transom is then installed on the aft end of the keel. If she is to be Round Bilge, molds which have already been made to conform to the shape the boat is to be, are placed every 4 or 5 feet apart, depending on the size of the boat. These are usually braced from overhead. If she is to be Lapstrake, she is now planked to these molds, bevelling the edge of the planks to follow the contour of the hull, with the planks overlapping each over about 7/8th of an inch and nailed together. When she is planked to the Sheer (gunwale) she is then ribbed.

If the boat is to be Carvel Planked or Smoothskin as commonly known, the procedure is a little different. In Carvell Planking, the planks are fitted edge to edge with a caulking seam at each joint, especially on the planking under water. Before we can start to plank a Smoothskin boat, we have to first rib her. (see photo number 2)

To rib her, ribbons or battens about 1-1/4 x 2 inches are fastened on to the Molds from Stem to Transom about 3 - 5 feet apart, depending on the sharpness of the curve of the bilge. After battens have been installed up to the Sheer, the steam-bent Ribs are put into place and clamped to the Battens. The batten next to the keel is then removed and first round or Garboard Plank is installed. When this round of planking is fastened to the ribs, the next batten is removed and the second round of planking is installed. This procedure is followed until the boat is planked to the Sheer. (see photo number 2)

If the boat is to be a Vee bottom, after the Keel, Stem and Transom have been installed on the Stock, all the permanent Frames are set up on the Keel and the Chines are installed. Then the Topsides are planked to Sheer and fastened into the permanent Frames which are spaced from 2 feet in distance apart, depending on boat size. She is then removed from the Stock and turned over and the Bottom installed. This type of boat is often set up-side-down with Sheer line marked acurately on the Frames and this baseline used to set the right line for the height of the Frames; then after the Chines are installed, both the Bottom and Topsides can be installed.

From here on, construction is about the same on all types of boats. First, as they say, the "guts" are put in; they are the Longtitudinal Stringers running from the transom to a few feet from the bow, and depending on the size of the boat, placed about a foot on either side of the Keel and are often used as the engine bed or have separate pieces of wood bolted on to the sides to serve as an engine bed or support to hold up the engine. Along with these Stringers there are usually several low Crossers or Bulkheads that bolt through the Frames or Ribs to secure the whole works to the bottom of the boat.

Now the Arrangement Plan can be set out and all floor beams, floors, seats, deck beams, decking can be installed. As soon as guts, clamp strakes and deck beams are installed, the boat is sufficiently braced and now can be moved around so the bottom and topsides can be planed, scraped and sanded. This is a major operation and one which establishes the reputation of the builder. A well-built boat with attractive lines is ruined if the finish on the wood looks as though it had been done with a rasp.

The decking on most Muskoka built boats is usually narrow strips of mahogany about 5/8 inches thick and 1-3/4 inches wide with a groove cut on one edge to receive a composition filler to set the deck off (usually white or yellow). After the woodwork is completed and sanded the boat is ready to be stained if she is made of mahogany. Most builders had their own special man who was an expert at this job; he could mix a stain which would colour the wood as uniformly as possible. The boat was then given 5 to 8 coats of Varnish applied with a brush, sanding between each coat or more coats if necessary.

The bigger shops had their own upholsterer, while independent upholsterers kept busy doing this work for several builders. All upholstery was made from real leather, the hides being ordered in the colour chosen by the customer.

Muskoka boats were usually built with the best grades of material available. White Oak and Phillipine Mahogany are good for the keel. White Oak for ribs; white oak or Phillipine Mahogany for sawn frames. Cedar or Cyprus for bottoms if single-skin; Phillipine Mahogany for twoply bottoms. Honduras and African Mahogany is best for Topsides and decks.

While some builders made their own patterns for deck hardware and had their own foundries, others sent their work out to be cast and plated. However, there has always been a good supply of quality deck hardware, casting and plating available to builders.

"How good we can make it", is our motto.
Not: "How cheap we can sell it".

DITCHBURN

A complete book could very easily be devoted to the story of the Ditchburn Boat Works. From the early 1870s until 1938 they built a great many boats, from 10-foot yacht tenders to 120-foot cruisers. The company employed hundreds of hands during its 65 years of operation in the works in Gravenhurst and Orillia, not to mention their various branches, depots and showrooms in Montreal, Brockville, Toronto, Georgian Bay, as well as Rosseau, Windermere, Port Carling and Beaumaris on these lakes.

The earliest catalogue we have found illustrates their models from about 1908 featuring everything from canoes to 45-foot day cruisers. During the next 30 years the production of cruisers was to become increasingly important to the firm until, in 1925, a new, larger works was built in Orillia to handle orders for boats of more than 50 feet in length for customers off the Muskoka Lakes. From Orillia, boats could be launched directly into the Trent-Severn Waterway for delivery anywhere on the Great Lakes. The dimensions of the boats were no longer constrained by the size of a railway flat car; they could now be built to a maximum dictated by the locks on the Trent. Cruisers of quite extraordinary beauty and luxury were built — dozens of them — for such influential patrons as the Eatons, Duffs, Fulfords, Kilgours — the list goes on.

Some of these yachts sold for in excess of $100 thousand (pre-inflation dollars). Ditchburn also contracted on several occasions for the building of sizeable patrol boats for the Federal Government.

William Ditchburn, naval advisor to Queen Elizabeth at the time of the Spanish Armada.

Henry Ditchburn, founder of the present industry at Gravenhurst, Muskoka.

Herbert Ditchburn, president of Ditchburn Boats, Limited, and internationally known as a master boat designer and builder.

The schooner yacht, Volna, built for the Grand Duke Constantine of Russia in 1858 in the Ditchburn yards at Blackwall, England.

The Blackwall frigate, Cospatrick, on which Henry Ditchburn, founder of the Canadian yards, sailed as a midshipman between London and the Orient.

A typical production of the Ditchburn yards of to-day—the Virginian II owned by Gordon Lefebvre, vice-president of General Motors, and in use on Lake Ontario.

BOAT BUILDERS FOR 500 YEARS

The Ditchburn family have been building boats for five hundred years. At the time of the Spanish Armada William Ditchburn was one of the naval advisors to Queen Elizabeth and three hundred years later his descendents were the pioneers in the construction of the first iron ship. Henry Ditchburn, founder of the present industry at Gravenhurst, Muskoka, sailed as a midshipman on the Blackwall frigate, Cospatrick, between London and the Orient for nine years before coming to Canada.

The head of today's organization, Herbert Ditchburn, began in the yards at 19 years of age his career which has brought him world wide recognition as a designer and builder of pleasure and speed craft.

1. An advertisement widely featured by Ditchburn.

2. Interior of the Shop at Gravenhurst about 1905.

We have quite arbitrarily skimmed over this aspect of Ditchburn's work, as we are primarily concerned with the classic launches synonymous with fine boating in Muskoka. To give you a taste of what sort of work Herb Ditchburn and Naval Architect Bert Hawker were turning out, we will illustrate a few of their larger craft, but the reader must bear in mind that by 1930 their production of launches was very much the smaller division of the company's sales; the production of custom cruisers had become the forte of Ditchburn.

In 1869, four of the Ditchburn brothers, William, Henry, John and Arthur, emigrated to Muskoka from England, settling in Rosseau. John eventually moved to Toronto, leaving his three brothers in the village on the new Ontario frontier. With the building of Pratt's hotel in Rosseau, a demand for boats developed. The Ditchburns started to build rowboats and canoes in the upper storey of William's house. By 1874 the brothers had a fleet of 24 rowboats in their livery; these were rented to tourists on a daily or weekly basis.

The Ditchburns came from a long line of shipwrights; they had established a works in England at the time of the Great Armada. Henry had served in the Royal Navy and during the 1870s established himself as the leading boatman in Muskoka.

While there were a number of others building small craft in Muskoka — Hall at Port Sandfield, Henry in Bracebridge, Scott in Gravenhurst and, more significantly, Johnston in Port Carling — Henry Ditchburn was the most prominent, with depots at Rosseau, Gravenhurst, Port Carling, Port Cockburn and on Georgian Bay. He was referred to in tourist literature of the day as the "ubiquitous Mr. Ditchburn", with his boats and camping equipment to be found wherever a tourist sojourned.

Ditchburn 25 foot.

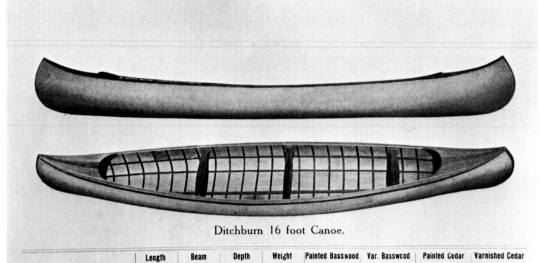

Ditchburn 16 foot Canoe.

PRICE LIST	Length	Beam	Depth	Weight	Painted Basswood	Var. Basswood	Painted Cedar	Varnished Cedar
	15	28	11	55	$24.00	$31.00	$35.00	$40.00
Including 2 Paddles	16	30	12	65	28.00	35.00	40.00	44.00
	16	31	13	70	29.00	37.00	42.00	45.00
with each Canoe:	17	34	14	82	34.00	41.00	45.00	49.00
	18	36	16	90	38.00	46.00	51.00	56.00

Family Rowboat

WE claim this to be the most efficient and safest boat for family use on the market to-day, being the result of many tests and a careful study. It is very steady on the water and a light-rowing boat for its size. Will seat comfortably six persons. Can be made in same style up to 20 feet long, or built with square stern. Weight about 175 lbs. **Construction**—Planking 7-16 Northern cedar; ribs ⅞ half round white oak, spaced 7 inches; stems, keel and gunwhale white oak; trimmed with butternut and cherry; finished with three coats best spar varnish. Equipped with two pairs of spoon blade spruce oars, three backs for seats, and rudder. Price complete $55.00. EXTRAS—Finished in mahogany with nickle-plated fittings $10. Best plush cushions $12. Pantisote or rexine cushions $10. Built with square stern $10.

Our Power Skiff.

A very popular and inexpensive Power Boat. Ideal for fishing purposes. Light enough to be pulled into an ordinary boathouse by one man. Can be easily loaded on a wagon and portaged from one lake to another, or can be shipped by freight at low cost. Can be run in very shallow water, or easily rowed if desired. Is seaworthy enough to weather anything that blows in most Canadian inland lakes. Will carry four or five persons and has a speed of 6½ miles per hour. Construction similar to that of rowboats, having much fuller lines, is deeper, wider and stronger. Length over all, 16 ft.; depth midship, 16 in.; depth forward, 24 in.; depth aft at transom, 11 in. Planking, 7-16 in. cedar; ribs, 1 in. half round white oak, spaced 6 in. Equipped with a 2 h.p. engine, with reversing blade propeller; one pair of oars, rudder, and otherwise equipped ready to run. Prices: Best grade and varnished, $185.00; painted inside and out, $175.00; waterproof duck cover (extra), $6.00.

3 - 8 Illustrations of Ditchburn boats from a catalogue published c 1908.

Cabin Day Cruiser

Realizing they were situated on the wrong end of the Lakes, the Ditchburns moved to Gravenhurst in the Muskoka Wharf area in 1890. There is a tantalizing reference in a Gravenhurst paper dated 1922 to Henry's building the first gasoline launch in Muskoka in Gravenhurst in 1893. It states that in that year he saw his first motorboat in the waters off Gravenhurst (the boat had been brought up from Toronto) and decided to build one for himself. He also organized his business as an unincorporated company: the H. Ditchburn Co. While this was a propitious move, it does not appear much came of it for several years, as he did not start building motorboats in any number until 1898.

Among Henry's employees in the 1890s was Tom Greavette, who was joined a few years later by Henry's nephew, Herb Ditchburn. By 1904 Herb was running the Gravenhurst operation, later buying out his uncle Henry's interest. In June 1907 the business was incorporated with the new Directors being Herbert and Alfred Ditchburn and Thomas Greavette. Within a few years Henry retired completely from the new enterprise. He died in 1912.

The newly organized H. Ditchburn Boat Manufacturing Co. Ltd. of Gravenhurst put out a beautifully-produced, 24-page illustrated catalogue presenting their various lines. Even at this early date the company offered a full range of power boats, described as good ''all round'' launches; safe for women and children and ''handsome enough to suit the most fastidious''. The literature noted that Ditchburn had been building launches powered by gasoline engines since 1898, and in 1908 offered a line of boats ranging from a 16-foot powered skiff, to a 45-foot day cruiser. And it added the proviso: ''If you do not see what you want, ask for it. We do not know what you want, but we can build what you need''.

GRAVENHURST ARCHIVES COMMITTEE

9. An early launch.

10 Employees c 1920.

11. A typical launch that figured in advertisements in 1915. Note the top.

In keeping with a tradition that was to hold true throughout the history of the company, customers were invited to visit the shop. At any time they could personally view the construction of their boat, from the time it was laid out to delivery, to satisfy themselves that their order was being filled with, "honest material and honest workmanship" — a combination guaranteed to bring satisfaction.

While it was estimated (and in all likelihood over-estimated) that in 1910 there were several hundred power boats on the Muskoka Lakes, we can say with confidence that the vast majority of them were brought onto the lakes from Toronto, Brantford, Hamilton, and especially from the U.S.A. No one in Muskoka was building launches on a great scale. H.C. Minett was building at Minett well before this time, as well as Henry and his nephew Herb Ditchburn, and doubtless a few others. But the Canadian marques that were best known were builders such as Jutten and Bastien of Hamilton and Schofield-Holden of Toronto. Launch building really came into its own in the first years of this century, even though launches were being commercially produced in the late 1880s and early 1890s. Many entrepreneurs entered into the business, only to fall by the wayside in a very few years as a handful of firms flourished, establishing themselves as the standard for others to match.

In Muskoka, boat builders achieved a local pre-eminence by the First World War and within the next 15 years established a nationwide reputation. The firm that was directly responsible for this was Ditchburn's.

From the time of incorporation to 1921, Ditchburn staff increased from seven or eight to just less than 30 hands. The production of rowboats, canoes and sailing dinghies — the mainstay of the business from 1870 — was virtually a thing of the past by 1921, as orders for launches and cruisers came in ever increasing numbers.

12. Tom Greavette in 23' launch 1921.

13. 36' launch 1921.

14. Ditchburn employees 1921.

The old two-storey boat house in Gravenhurst — the main branch of Henry Ditchburn's network of boat liveries that had been founded in Rosseau a half-century before had been substantially renovated to cope with new demands on both production and size of boat ordered.

The shop was originally located at the foot of Muskoka Wharf, which at the time it was built (c 1890) was the prime location in Muskoka; all tourist trade was funnelled by rail to Gravenhurst to connect with the Navigation Company steamers. Hundreds of people de-trained there daily during the season and it was by far the busiest spot in the District. Some time before the Great War, Herb Ditchburn bought a large stable from the Crossley's Sandy Bay Farm near Morgan's Bay close to the village of Rosseau. The timbers from this shed were brought to Gravenhurst and an addition built around them on the spit in Gravenhurst Bay next to Muskoka Wharf Station (adjacent to the all-important rail siding). Here the company built boats until August 1915, when the plant was destroyed by fire and replaced by a brick factory building on the same site. The latter is still standing: some of the timbers that were salvaged from the old shop were incorporated in the ceiling of Sloan's Restaurant in Gravenhurst.

One of the first boats built in the new brick shop was probably the best known and largest of the Ditchburn boats built during the 'teens: the KAWANDAG II. She was built during the shop's first winter before electric lighting was installed and, as the late Roscoe Groh remembered, the length of the working day was determined by the amount of daylight; as the spring wore on, the longer the day at the plant!

KAWANDAG II, built for John (later Sir John) Eaton, was designed by Bowes & Mower. Powered by twin eight-cylinder Sterling engines, she was capable of a speed of 24 m.p.h. despite

15. A 31 ft. standard displacement launch - painted hull.

16. A 36ft. standard displacement launch - mahogany hull.

17. PROHIBITION - 36' hardchine Ditchburn built for J.H. Hillman, Gibralter Island, Lake Muskoka, 1922. Powered by GRS 6 cylinder Sterling. Speed 38 mph.

her size (she was 73 feet by 12 feet). Built entirely of select mahogany, the KAWANDAG II was the first "big" boat built by Ditchburn — and must rank as one of the finest. To call her a boat is a misnomer; she was a yacht — beautifully finished and appointed (as these photos attest) — as was only fitting for one of the premier families of Canada's commercial aristocracy. KAWANDAG II remained on the Muskoka Lakes until 1938, at which time she was sold to someone from the Detroit area. Her fate is unknown.

The KAWANDAG was followed a few years later by another "showcase" boat: the 61 foot cruiser IDYLESE, built for Col. T.A. Duff of Toronto. This boat was designed by Bert Hawker after joining the firm on his return from Great War service with the 122nd Battalion, Canadian Expeditionary Force. Powered by an 8-cylinder Sterling, it maintained a speed of 18 m.p.h. and was a very elegant harbinger of what was to become the main thrust of Ditchburn's business in the decade to follow: the construction of very sizeable, elegant and powerful cruisers for the North American market.

Ditchburn's plant in 1922 covered one and one-half acres. With their staff of close to 30 men they were building up to 18 launches in a year, from 18 to 45 feet in length. But the preeminent boat on the stocks was the DOLLY DURKIN, under construction for the Eaton family. She had been ordered by Sir John shortly before his sudden passing and was considered by Herb Ditchburn the finest boat ever to emerge from his works to that time. Powered by a 275 H.P. Sterling engine, the 38-foot launch was capable of 36 m.p.h. Built entirely of mahogany, with aluminum and nickel-plated fixtures, it was described in the local press as "too good to be true". In August of that year, two Ditchburn boats raced in the Fisher Gold Cup Races; these were Harry Greening's RAINBOW II, and T.A.

18 - 20 KAWANDAG II

Duff's IONIC III, the later driven by Bert Hawker. With ever-increasing sales spurred on by that consummate salesman, Tom Greavette, and the attendant publicity of building Harry Greening's RAINBOWS the plant was doubled in size in 1923. Within a year, the work force had risen to more than 60 men and the firm was faced with orders for boats too large to be built in Gravenhurst; a new plant was built in Orillia.

In 1926, the Ditchburn works in Gravenhurst and Orillia employed more than 133 men, and better than one-half the value of company production was being exported to the United States. This last point was a matter of particular pride to Herb Ditchburn — and indeed to the whole community — as only 15 years before a very significant proportion of the boats sold in Muskoka were imported from south of the border.

Publicity is, of course, the best advertisement any manufacturer can ask for. In addition to Ditchburn's connection with Mr. Greening's famous racing career they built one boat for a customer in Vancouver in 1928. In July of 1928 the MISS VANCOUVER left the Severn (where it had been transported by Bill Cameron who transported all Ditchburn's small boats from Gravenhurst) embarking on an all-water trip around the U.S. and through the Panama Canal to Vancouver. She made the trip without incident — but not without lots of press coverage!

One of the services we take for granted today is a ready supply of gasoline; there are independent marinas situated at convenient spots throughout the lakes that will service and store motorboats. Years ago, of course, this was not the case; the day of the independent operator who would service motorboats, supply gasoline, oil, and make mechanical repairs did not dawn until the 1920s. Before that time, the engine manufacturer would send his own shop-based mechanic up from the city, or staff from the boat builder would be sent to effect repairs on the

21. Head on view of 36' Vee bottom, built for Carl Read. Sister ship of PROHIBITION.

22. A 21' runabout, 1922.

23. DOLLY DURKIN 38' 1922.

COMMODORE H.B. GREENING

Harry Greening was one of the best known and most influential men in boating between the wars. His first power boat was a canoe in which he installed a homemade 3 h.p. engine, built in his attic on a foot lathe. Between 1908 and 1919 he owned a series of speed boats named GADFLY. With his first boat named RAINBOW in 1920, Greening started competing seriously here and in the United States. He had Ditchburn build him a new, more advanced and technologically innovative boat practically every year. The RAINBOWS culminated in the U-70 or RAINBOW VII. Built in 1928, 38 feet long with a beam of 9 feet and powered with 1200 h.p. in two units, she won the Lipton Trophy in Detroit - carrying eight people!

1. H.B. Greening in RAINBOW I winning the Fisher Trophy, September 1920. She was designed by George Crouch, built by Ditchburn and powered with a dual valve 6 cylinder Sterling.

2. RAINBOW IV, a Gold Cup class boat built in 1924.

3. Harry Greening at the Muskoka Assembly at start of the 24 hour endurance run September 18, 19, 1923. RAINBOW III ran the 19-1/2 mile course on Lake Rosseau raising the existing 24 hour record 300 miles to 1064.

spot. Ditchburn, for instance, maintained depots at Point au Baril and Brockville, as well as Rosseau, Port Carling and Beaumaris on the Lakes. Teams of mechanics and woodworkers would be immediately dispatched to handle troubles wherever they took place — a follow-up service that was required and expected of any reputable firm. In addition, Ditchburn maintained a livery as well as offering a jitney service. Through the 'teens and early 1920s Bill Croucher one of his drivers, ran two boats from Gravenhurst: the HAPPY DAYS and the FAIRBANKS.

There are a number of references to be found in correspondence from the first decade of this century to orders placed from all over the lakes with Ditchburn for gasoline. The gasoline was delivered in barrels or five-gallon cans to the individual boat owner. Before Imperial Oil put their first supply boat on the lakes, gas was transported by tank car to Gravenhurst, where it was transferred to holding tanks at wharf-side via a pipeline. As orders came through from up the lakes, it was pumped by hand into barrels that lined a runway at wharf-side then manually transferred to a scow. Jimmy Campbell scowed the barrels around the lakes for years with his steamboats: the NYMPH, and later the CONSTANCE. After the C.N.O.R. built their line up the west side of the Lakes and built Lake Joseph Station at Barnesdale, Joe Bastien — a boatbuilder from Hamilton who operated a number of liveries on the upper two lakes — sold gas at the Barnesdale wharf. His holding tanks were under the wharf and apparently none too water-tight. Any gas purchased from Bastien was first pumped into five-gallon cans and then carefully filtered through a chamois or an old felt hat; not exactly an environmentally sound process!

After Imperial Oil put their first ''tanker'' on the lakes in the mid-1920s, gas was shipped through Bala on the C.P.R., and John Walker and George Black would travel from cottage to

27. DIX, 22' 1926 built for Dick Clemson now owned by James Woodruff.

28. B-1V. Built for Carl Borntraeg of Cinderwood Island, Lake Muskoka and now owned by Gord Wilson. Photographed at the M.L. Country Club, 1935.

cottage refilling individual holding tanks. However, the day of the entrepreneur peddling gas was not gone: John C. Gray remembers well Captain Charles Woodroffe of Footes Bay scowing B.A. Peerless gasoline with his steamer, the VOYAGEUR. His recollection of the old, wood-burning steamer throwing sparks from its stack, while his father and Charlie Woodroffe enjoyed a cigar in the process of pumping gasoline into a dozen five gallon cans to be stored under the cottage, is not a comfortable one. Tempting fate was how things were done in the ''good old days'' and this, if nothing else, helps explain how so many boat-houses were burned.

During conversation with almost anyone intimately involved in boat building in its hey-day in the 1920s, the point will be made that H.C. Minett went to extraordinary (some pointedly say ridiculous) lengths to build perfect boats. Over and over again the opinion is expressed: that Bert Minett could not build a boat to a price if he wanted to, while Herb Ditchburn could and did. That is not to say that the Ditchburn works did not turn out excellent work — the results speak for themselves; its standards of design, construction, finishing and engine installation were extremely high.

Charles Amey of Port Carling worked for Ditchburn in the winter of 1926-'27 and his recollection of the experience is a telling one. Mr. Amey has been a boat-builder for more than 60 years; he started with John Matheson, worked for the Disappearing Propeller Boat Co., the Port Carling Boat Works, Murdon Marine, and is now building custom skiffs in his own shop. To this day, Charlie is impressed with the quality of work done in the Ditchburn shop. The concentration of craftsmen in Gravenhurst in the 1920s was unique; almost all company staff members were local men — something in excess of seventy in Gravenhurst and a number more at the Orillia works.

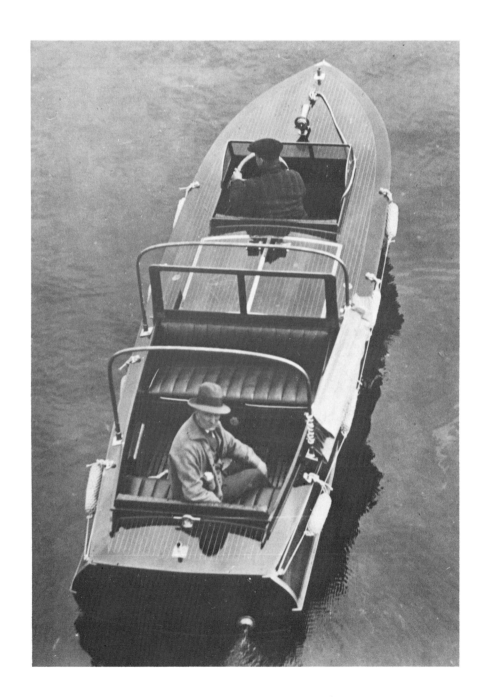

29. *Yacht Tender 23' built in 1927 for Sam McLaughlin.*

30. *BLYTHEWOOD III - 37' built 1927 of vermillion wood, for the McLaughlin family of Oshawa and Sunnyside Island, Lake Rosseau. Now owned by C. Herman, Lake Joseph.*

31. *Ewart McLaughlin in the WHIPPET, 1929.*

The main shop in 1926 was a very busy place indeed. There were up to half a dozen boats set up on stocks at any given time. One foreman or master builder, together with two, three or four helpers — depending on the size of the boat — would take an order and work on it, from the setting up until the hull was planked and ribbed ready to be decked and finished. A few other men were busy at all times getting out materials for them. Bert Hawker, designer and plant superintendent, divided his time between Gravenhurst and Orillia, overseeing the work very closely, working with the individual foremen and following each order through. Herb Ditchburn, in addition to all his other responsibilities as the president of a firm employing upward of 130 hands, still made his presence felt on the shop floor, making daily tours throughout the works.

In an operation of this size, which was far larger than anything else at this time in the country, one would expect that "efficiency experts" would have made their mark, demanding 'x' amounts of results from a given amount of labour; the imposition of a standard production rate with a minimum threshold of quality that had to be met. This was not the case. If one man could do a job in four hours and another took six, the slower was not chided, as long as his work was of the best and the end result was in keeping with the high standard of workmanship demanded by Ditchburn.

This attention to detail — to doing things right — to building a good, strong, tight, attractive launch or cruiser made for a reputation that carried the Ditchburn marque from coast to coast in the Dominion and south of the border to Florida.

As we have seen, Ditchburn had begun to build a line of hard chine vee-bottom boats of from 21 to 36 feet in length in 1921 on lines taken off the first of Harry Greening's famous RAINBOW. This bottom was designed by

BALA REGATTA - 1933

Opposite Page -
32. *LLANO, Ditchburn 37 ft. built 1918 for Wm. Irwin and now owned by Mr. Irwin Miller at Llanlar, Windermere. Originally gasoline powered but changed to Cumming diesel around 1928. Cumming had previously worked for Mr. Wm. Irwin in the U.S.A.*

33. *A 31' launch built in 1925. Today owned by Ed Skinner.*

George F. Crouch of New York State and, as was the case with so many builders up here, one bottom was used over and over again, scaled up or down to suit the models ordered, and the topside reworked to suit a very demanding and sophisticated clientele. For the next half dozen years, however, the bulk of the production of launches was made up of standard Hawker designed displacement launches.

In 1927, John Ringling of Sarasota, Florida commissioned a 28-foot racing boat from Ditchburn; the SILVER QUEEN. It would appear that this was the genesis of what became one of the most popular models to come out of the works from 1928 to 1931, the "Viking". This hard, chine-stepped hull was well received from the very beginning and was featured in most of the advertisements of the day. Today there are still a number of these launches on the lakes, most notably the MOWITZA and the BETTY MAC (now known as the FLIP-A-COIN). Several dozen launches were constructed on these lines in the late 1920s as the works were expanded yet again. Concurrent with the introduction of the Viking model was the development of a new, larger model of launch, the 31-foot "Commodore".

These models reflected a new look in styling that was coming into vogue. There was a shift away from the long, low, uncluttered displacement launch that had been the hallmark of boat building from the time of the Great War; now the look was a little more "racy". Low freeboards were still the rule of the day, but with engines of higher horse-power and over-head camshafts, it became necessary to raise the hatches to accommodate this extra height. Hatches were no longer flush with the mahogany decks but raised with a series of scooped ventilators running down their sides; windshields were installed on both forward and rear cockpits and the lines were harder, achieving an overall impression of power and speed.

35. *FLIP-A-COIN in the locks, Port Carling.*

36. *BOB BET II, a 31' Commodore built for Roy Moodie 1928.*

37. *MOWITZA II, a 27' Viking built 1929 for Fred Burgess.*

Production of launches during these years — as the countdown began for the Crash and Great Depression that was to mark the denouement for Ditchburn — was not limited to these two models. A number of traditional displacement boats were still built, as the public was by no means unanimous on what they wanted in a launch. A significant proportion of the buying public did not want anything to do with all the "splutter fuss" of the planing boats; they were content to move along at a respectable speed and not willing to sacrifice the easy ride of a long narrow hull cutting through the water in an admittedly very elegant fashion. Large livery launches such as the LADY ELGIN — built for Captain Wallace of Minett in 1927 — were still in demand, as was the custom work that was the result of the patronage of the racing aficionados — the Greenings and Carstairs of this world. In January 1930 Ditchburn operated a city sales office at 108 King St. W. in Toronto. The 28-foot Viking, 31-foot Commodore, and the new 24-foot forward drive "Neptune" model were displayed, along with Peterborough, Dispro and Port Carling Boat Works models.

As in every sector of the economy, the Great Depression severely affected the boating industry. Small boat orders fell off drastically in 1930 in both Canada and the U.S., and Ditchburn's had its first major layoff in July. The Gravenhurst paper bemoaned the fact that when, in November of that year, an order was finally taken for a cruiser, it was too big for the Gravenhurst plant — so there was no work in town and the local men had to go to Orillia to be employed. This may have provided some (ill-founded) consolation in the belief that the order was indicative of a revival in the boating industry.

The situation for Ditchburn in 1931 became even more difficult in April, when Greavette's was put into operation, vying with them for

38. A Ditchburn advertisement used in the late 1920s.

39. Henry Buttler in his 1930 24' Neptune.

40. Two displacement launches at Gravenhurst Antique Boat Show 1977. The BRICIE owned by Bruce Evans and the WASAN - Glen S. Coates owner.

small-boat orders. Through 1931 some small boat orders were taken, but the plant in Gravenhurst was only working at a fraction of its capacity; more than two thirds of the employees had been laid off and many that remained were busy fabricating parts for the two big boat orders being handled in Orillia. Those two orders, however — one an 85-foot houseboat for the Lake of the Woods and the other a 117-foot patrol boat for the Dominion Government — would only keep Orillia busy until the fall. There was nothing else on the books for the winter of 1931.

In 1931 everything fell apart and in the spring of '32 the 60-year-old Ditchburn enterprise reached the nadir of its fortunes and collapsed entirely. It is not difficult today to picture the tumultuous negotiating that went on between Herb Ditchburn and his creditors during those trying months. On the 10th of May, 1932, it appeared that he had managed to salvage something of the business when at a meeting held at E.R.C. Clarkson's offices in Toronto with his creditors, it was determined to continue for another six months under new management. R.P. Powell was to take charge of the business, assisted by A.H. Hawker — Herb Ditchburn to be responsible for sales. Something happened within a few days of this arrangement being made and on the 26th of May the company was adjudged bankrupt.

On November 10, 1932 the *Gravenhurst Banner* published a letter from Herb Ditchburn wherein he tried to explain what had happened to his business and to the boating industry in general. The dust was only beginning to settle after the dramatic failure of his enterprise following a decade of rapid expansion. The figures that he offered graphically tell the story: in 1930, 425 motorboats were produced in all of Canada, worth a total of less than $1½ million. The following year, 254 motorboats were produced, with a value of just $500 thousand. This repre-

sented a decrease of about 40 percent and a decrease in the net value of construction of fully 65 percent. This was spread around 120 different boat manufacturing enterprises. The outlook for 1932 was even grimmer and the general feeling was that the trend would continue in 1932 and sales for the industry as a whole would amount to only $185,000.

As Herb pointed out, while Ditchburn produced over 40 percent of the value of the entire output of the industry in Canada in 1931, the market was simply too small to keep the business in profitable operation. Four years previously, Ditchburn produced 25 percent of all boats in Canada — so they had increased their market share significantly — but the volume was not there.

The heavy investment in the large plant and equipment in the previous decade, most recently in the expansion of 1929, made with the expectation of ever increasing sales, was simply too much to carry.

Within a few months rumours circulated through town that the irrepressible Mr. Ditchburn was attempting to resurrect something from the ashes and intended to resume operation on a much reduced scale in the old plant. He had been relieved of the intolerable burden of debt that had become the bane of the old company. On March 9th, 1933, some 10 months after the failure, a new company was incorporated; the Ditchburn Boat & Yachting Co. Ltd. So Ditchburn was back in business on a much reduced scale in the old plant. A new line of launches was introduced, aimed at a different market. Stock boats of from 18 to 24 feet in length offered both clinker and smooth skin that would appeal to a lower price market. The idea had been to build caskets as well in the plant, utilizing the excess capacity, but whether anything along this line was ever done is not known.

43. *POPEYE II, 1934.*

44. *Ditchburn hull finished by Port Carling Boat Works after sale of the Company's assets.*

During this period of the 30's, Herb Ditchburn designed a stern-drive similar to the one used on inboard/outboards which are so popular today. It operated with a short shaft between the engine and stern-drive. Ditchburn installed the device in a standard design hull which would normally have had the engine farther forward, but the launch didn't have enough width at the stern to carry the load, so it just ploughed through the water. The experiment was therefore discontinued.

Some custom work was done and a few 225 class boats were built; the two best known were the ATOM built for Harry 'Red' Foster, and the POPEY, driven by Herb Ditchburn Jr. at the C.N.E. in 1934. While a few cruisers were built, the largest being the 52-foot BIRCH BARK in 1935, more financial difficulties were encountered and the company was reorganized one last time as the Ditchburn Boat and Aircraft Co. (1936) Ltd., but this company failed as well in the summer of 1938 when the bank called a loan of $10 thousand. Bill Ogilvie who handled the sales of Ditchburn at the end, still thinks that the bank's action was both premature and unjustified as operations were picking up satisfactorily. He believes that with time, the company would have re-established its niche in the market.

As it was, this last failure marked the end of a five year struggle to salvage the company and Herb Ditchburn left the business in Gravenhurst for good. After a brief stint in the boat brokerage business he became involved in war work in Trenton with Gar Wood. He died in 1950, leaving a legacy of hundreds of beautifully-crafted cruisers and launches, many of which are still the pride of Canada's inland waters.

MINETT AND MINETT SHIELDS

*"Built for those who are not satisfied
with ordinary standards"*

Half a century ago there were many fine boatbuilders in Muskoka, but there was one man gen-
erally considered by his contemporaries as being
at the top of the list: H.C. (Bert) Minett. The
boats turned out by Minett's shop rank among
the finest — both from the point of view of construction and from a simple esthetic standard.
His boats are extremely pleasing to the eye. As a
rule they are each in their own right an 'individual'; each stands alone, custom-built, reflecting
the ever-developing art of the builder and the
particular desire of the contracting buyer.

While the occasional launch is found as far
afield as California, the bulk of his production at
that time went to the Muskoka Lakes and Lake of
Bays, and that is where most of his surviving
boats are found today. No records of his production have survived, but it would appear that he
did not build any more than 250 boats — of
which a relatively large number are still in exis-
tence.

The story of Minett's boat building can be divided, like Gaul, into three parts; his work on
Lake Rosseau from the late 1890s, the establishment of the H.C. Minett Motor Boat Works in
Bracebridge in 1910, and lastly, the formation of
Minett-Shields Ltd. in 1925. For all intents and
purposes, the active operations of the firm
ceased in 1948, though some work was done
until 1953 and the company's charter was not
surrendered for another five years.

Hubert Charles Minett was born on the family farm in 1881. This farm was to become the
well known summer resort Clevelands House at

1. Bert (left) and Arthur Minett on canopy of Steamer MINETA c 1905.

2. MAGIC 24' x 4', built about 1905. Bert Minett is at the controls, Art and his wife in the stern.

3. An earlier MINETA than the boat known by that name on the lakes today. This boat was built c. 1914.

Minett P.O. Lake Rosseau. While a teenager, Bert started building boats in an old outbuilding behind the hotel. He used locally cut white pine, which, according to all accepted wisdom, should rot quickly. However, the first motor boat that he built, for E.R. Wood, is still in relatively good condition. Owned today by a well known boating enthusiast, James Woodruff, she is in the process of being restored. Another of his early boats was an 18-foot open cockpit launch with a one lunger Ferro-Sterlington Make & Break Engine built for John Eaton and used in later years by Thorel House on Lake Rosseau. It is thought that both of these boats were built before 1900 with the help of Bert's brother S.A. (Arthur) Minett. Undoubtedly, a number of others were built as Bert gained proficiency in the trade and by 1902 or 1903 he built a 45-foot steam launch, the MINETA, on the beach at Clevelands House.

Over the next seven years Minett built several more launches while working at the hotel. At one point, he left Muskoka for Alganac, Michigan, where he worked for John L. Hacker. After spending a couple of years with Hacker, establishing a connection with this famous marine architect and builder, he went to Boston, where he became quite friendly with the well-known sailboat architect, Stevenson. Bert is thought to have built only one sailboat, a 30-foot sloop for Arthur Hardy (her unique boat house is still a landmark on Ouno Island on Lake Rosseau).

In December, 1910, Bert went into business in a bigger way, moving to Bracebridge and setting up shop as The H.C. Minett Motor Boat Works. The new enterprise was located on the ground floor of a substantial building, formerly a chair factory of the Hess Furniture Company. By this time, the building was owned by Mr. George Tennant a prominent lumberman in town. Northern Planing Mills now occupy the site.

4. PEGGY built for Mrs. J.S. Brown of Beaumaris and Pittsburgh. Albert Lawson drove this boat for many years.

5. NORWOOD II going 32 m.p.h.

Among the first boats he built was the NOR-WOOD II. Built in 1911 for W.L. Clause of Norwood Lodge, Lake Joseph and Pittsburg, this 31-foot launch is still the pride and joy of Barbara Devens, granddaughter of Mr. Clause. Built entirely of mahogany (instead of Ontario cedar and mahogany, as was the rule in those days) she is long and — to our eyes — extraordinarily narrow. NORWOOD II was also reputed to be the fastest launch on the lakes until 1914 when G.V. Foreman of Cliff Island, Lake Joseph and Buffalo, commissioned from Bert a 32-foot boat with a cedar hull.

Designed with a wider stern to keep the bow down, and powered with a 6-cylinder Van Blerck, TANGO proved the faster and was the fastest on the lakes for some time. Named for that risque dance that was sweeping the country just before the war, this launch was built for $2500, a formidable price for those days and indicative of the quality of the materials and amount of labour that went into her.

It is interesting to see just how much society has changed in the past 70 years. When new, the TANGO was operated by two uniformed men: a captain and an engineer; the passengers sat aft. As late as the 1930s it was not uncommon to see one of these old launches cutting down the lake with a uniformed chauffeur at the helm.

Another well-known Minett boat still on the lakes and equally well maintained is Dr. Bateman's RITA. This 50-foot cruiser was built in 1914 and purchased by Carl Borntraeger of Cinderwood Island, Beaumaris, for the sacrifice price of $7,500. A beautiful craft, she was the largest that Bert built in the old chair factory. Too large to team down to the town wharf and launch, she was shipped to Gravenhurst by rail and launched there.

Most of the boats Minett built up to 1932 were 28 to 36 feet in length, and until 1926 they were all round, bilge-displacement hulls. There

6. *Mr. and Mrs. H. Devens in NORWOOD II, the boat built for Mrs. Devens grandfather over 70 years ago.*

7. *RITA in 1977, Chas. Smith is seen on board with John Gillan of Beaumaris on the wharf.*

is some controversy over how much of these boats were Bert's design; it is thought that all his "bottoms" were from plans designed by George Crouch of New York State. Bert himself intimated that this was the case in conversation with Charles Wheaton in the 1950s.

Among the better known of his boats from the 'teens that are still regularly seen on the lakes, are the MINETA, the HILO and the COME 'N' GO.

Adam Swanson and Reg Boyes both started working for Bert Minett quite early in the game, as did Bert Hawker. Hawker had come to Muskoka from Hamilton in 1912 to work for Minett. He brought with him a name as both designer and builder. His best known was a 50-foot cruiser, the largest in Hamilton. It is thought that he drew up the plans for the RITA; he certainly worked on her and spent the better part of her first summer with her at Cinderwood Island. Hawker left Minett to join the C.E.F. in 1916, and when demobilized joined Ditchburn.

Bert Minett moved his works in 1923 from the old chair factory, to the old foundry located on the riverbank below the falls, allowing for much easier movement of boats from water to shop. Within two years the condition of the business was critical; wages of the six employees were six months in arrears; Minett was working himself into bankruptcy. Things only turned around when 25-year-old Bryson Shields bought into the business in 1925. In September of that year a new company was formed, Minett-Shields Co. Ltd.

Behind its beauty —
correct design
Beneath its surface —
skilled construction

MINETT 🐦 SHIELDS
LIMITED
BRACEBRIDGE · CANADA

9. HILO built for Mrs. Carlyle of Beaumaris in 1917. Presently owned by the Tennant Estate; Les Tennant, a life-long booster of H.C. Minett. Ted Reid and son Kirk are in the boat.

8. MINETA built in 1917 as a hotel livery boat for Clevelands House.

10, 11, 12. HOO DOO 24', built in 1927 for Chan Hamlin of Buffalo and Governor's Island. Lake Joseph.

Bryson was the son of T.H. Shields of Brampton. His mother was a Haggert, a family that had been summering at "Idyloak" on Lake Joseph from the late 1870s. Bryson spent every summer on the lake, developing a love for boating and gained an appreciation for Minett's work. His father had an early Minett launch the IDYLOAK, about 36 feet in length and built before 1914.

Bryson had one experience that was certainly an occasion for a 14-year-old boy. When the First World War started, he took Sir Robert Borden in their launch from the Royal Muskoka Hotel to Lake Joe Station to meet a special train that was to take the Prime Minister to Ottawa.

Bryson was educated at the Royal Military College in Kingston and had gone into business for a short time before becoming involved with Minett. Minett certainly needed the capital and it looked like an ideal partnership. They were adequately capitalized for once, with a combination of talents: Bert, to oversee the building, and Bryson to handle the financial and sales end of the business. The timing could not have been better. The market for custom boats was just entering a real boom; demand was great and there were a good number of families with the wherewithall to pay $6000 and up for a new launch. Advances in design and technology had resulted in a new look in boats; boats that carried larger power plants, boats with forward drive, boats with planing hulls. People wanted to upgrade and turn in their old slender displacement boats on the new models.

Minett-Shields enjoyed its golden period in the late 1920s, when up to 15 custom launches were being built each year. These boats ranged from 24 to 36 feet in length, both Vee and displacement-bottomed. This period culminated in the construction of two cruisers, 50 and 55 feet in length, coinciding with the devastating onset

13. SHENANGO, 30', 1928, built for H.S. Bradley who summered at the Royal Muskoka Hotel. Present owner is W.P. Snyder III of Columbia Island, Lake Muskoka and Pittsburgh.

14. PIXIE III built for Dr. Capon in the late '20s.

15. NANIWA, 36', 1929. The original owner, Mr. E.B. Whitcomb is at the controls.

of the Depression — and consequent drying up of orders for luxury launches.

The shop was still located in the old foundry on the river (where it remained until the end). Inside the main building would be from five to seven boats under construction. One boat builder and a couple of helpers would tackle each job, setting it up and working on her until she was planked and ribbed, getting out their own materials. Typically, each boat was a different size, each a different model. Bert had his own tools and, while overseeing all, worked along with the men. At this time there were about two dozen workers at the plant.

In addition to Bert, Bryson, and the office staff, the general foremen were two old employees, Reg Boyes, a Bracebridge native, and an old Scotsman, Adam Swanson. Among the hands were a group of Englishmen: Jake and Leo Dunn, Art Watson and Jim Garden. Bill Casey did most of the fine finishing and cabinetry work; Hugh Devrill, Ernie Dollimore and a man named Tuck, the varnishing. Joe Sutherland, Jim Froh and Les Goodfellow, together with the mechanics Orville Simmonds, Frank Bates and Joe Morland, completed the team.

The boats built during this period are of exceptional beauty and exemplify the drive to perfection that was the hallmark of Minett-Shields. Nothing was allowed out of the shop until they were satisfied that there was nothing that could be done to improve it. Tales abound of Bert having parts of boats torn apart and redone — properly. A 34-foot launch, the DIC DON was being built for the Boxers of Rockhaven Island, Lake Rosseau in 1928. In the contract, a delivery date was specified and a penalty clause inserted, yet Bert would not allow the boat out of the shop, even though it could have been finished on time, as he was not satisfied with the quality of the mahogany to be used for the engine hatches.

16. *EAGLET II, 36', 1927. Powered with her original 225 H.P. Hall Scott, she is one of the finest big launches on the lakes today. Dave Forman of Eagle island and Buffalo is at the controls. (Pages 51-52)*

17. *Employees in 1928. Left to right: John Dunn, George Cairns (bookkeeper), Adam Swanson, Leo Dunn, Art Watson.*

18, 19. *Views of the shop in 1941.*

Bert was himself much more than an expert woodworker. He designed and patented his own windshields, stems, struts and steering mechanism as well as his deck hardware.

The launches produced in those palmy days can be roughly divided into three groups: the big displacement boats; the 26-foot displacement boats; and the hard-chine Vee-bottom boats. This last group consisted of two models designed by John Hacker, one 24 feet in length and the other 26. The 24-foot boats were driven from the stern with one cockpit forward of the engine. The better known of these were the GLORY II, CAPRICE II and the first RADIO. Chan Hamlin's HOO DOO had the same bottom but the lines from the water-up were completely streamlined; the result was a very attractive runabout. Sometimes in the early 1930s it burned and was replaced by an exact replica.

The first of the 26-foot forward-drive boats was Craig's WACOUTTA II, built during the winter of 1926-'27. It was followed by Hutchinson's FLEETWOOD II and Irwin's LLAN LADY in the next couple of years. Powered with 200 H.P., 6-cylinder Scripps engines, they move along at 40 m.p.h. While the hulls of these boats are all similar, the topsides were all slightly different; when contracting for the FLEETWOOD, Dr. Hutchison, for example, used Craig's WACOUTTA as his model and itemized the changes he wanted in his boat.

A fair number of 26-foot displacement boats were built, many of them quite alike in appearance. They were probably introduced in the early 1920s but were built right through to at least 1930. The SEA HAWK, ONNALINDA and WASCANA are all good examples of this style of boat that are still in regular use on the Lakes.

The big "show piece" boats were anywhere from 28 to 36 feet in length. They had Minett's modified displacement hull. The bottom was flattened at the transom to improve stability and

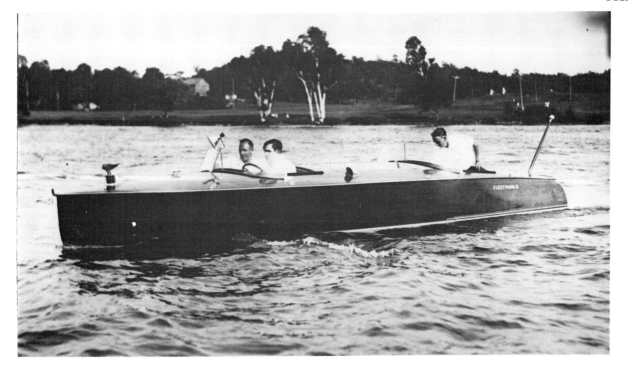

20, 21. GLORY II, 24', 1928. Built for Mr. Finch of Lake of Bays and Toronto, she was teamed up from Bracebridge.

22, 23 FLEETWOOD II, 26', 1929. Built for Dr. R.J. Hutchison, she is owned today by John C. Gray. Powered with the original 200 H.P. Scripps. Top view 1929, bottom 1984.

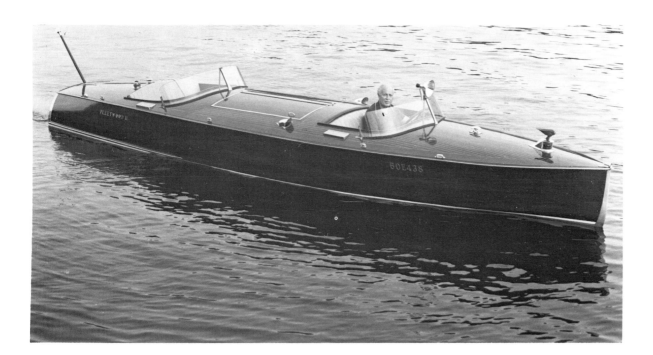

keep the bow down at speed. The list of these beautiful boats is relatively long and there is still a good number of them maintained in excellent condition on the lakes. Equipped with Minett's patented folding windshields in front of the driver and immediately in front of the stern seat; these boats achieved an elegance through economy of line, excellence in finish and detail that was rarely approached by anyone else. The NORWOOD III, EAGLET, MARMILWOOD, NANIWA, DIK DON, MARCO, SHENANGO and SEA HORSE all stand witness to this. There was one quite exceptional boat built for Mr. J.Y. Murdoch in 1929. The WIMUR was a 36-foot, two step hydroplane designed by Hacker. It was a one-off and featured widely in Minett-Shields' advertisements.

In 1930, the company landed contracts for two sizeable cruisers: the LOU, 50-foot long for Mr. Milne of the E.B. Eddy Co., and the MOBY DICK, 55-feet-long for Mr. Fulford of Brockville. These two orders represented a tremendous investment in time and money but were seen as the way of the future for the company. We only know of a few launches that date from this time: 32-foot, hard-chine, forward-drive boats; the GLEN AVY, SCUD II, and the JOLLY ROGER.

The '30s were a difficult period for Minett-Shields. After they finished the LOU and the MOBY DICK it does not appear that they had many, if any orders to fall back on. As was the case with Ditchburn, the market dried up, as everyone retrenched and a custom-built launch was naturally one luxury that could be put off. From the extensive advertising campaign the company embarked on in 1930, featuring their cruisers, it can be safely assumed that Bryson Shields was attempting to follow the path that Herb Ditchburn had pioneered 10 years before. The money was to be made with the "big" boat orders and in the boom of the late 1920s the market for

24, 26 WIMUR II. Built in 1929 for J.Y. Murdoch of Footes Bay and Toronto this 38' 2 step launch was widely featured in company publicity. She is currently owned by J.A.D. Gray of Port Cockburn and Port Credit.

25. SEA HAWK, 26', mid 1920s. Owned today by Tim Chisolm.

27, 28 Two views of the JOLLY
ROGER. Similar to the GLENAVY
and the SCUD. Bert Minett is in the
second cockpit.

29. ILLAWARRA II, 28' 1928.
Built for R.C. Breckinridge and
powered originally with a 125 H.P.
Kermath. She is owned today by
Doug Bassett.

cruisers was growing by leaps and bounds. The local market for Minett-Shields custom-built launches on the Muskoka Lakes and Lake of Bays was limited and the competition was increasing all the time. Full-page advertisements were run in the boating journals and Canadian Homes and Gardens illustrating the progress being made in their cruisers.

In conversation with just about anyone who had dealings with the company, there is one point that is invariably emphasized: Bryson Shields was a born salesman. An extremely personable young man, he had a way with the ladies, an enthusiasm for boating and, all the more importantly, the right connections. Altogether not a bad combination for selling on the lakes. He would take one of their latest launches and drive around, stopping at friends' and 'selling'. Although it worked wonderfully while people were buying, in the mid-'30s it was a different game; if the family had an old launch and did not need a new one then why not update it? Turn their old centre-drive boat into a new, stylish forward-drive?

In at least two cases his approach worked and A.K. Andrews of Sullivan Island, Lake Joseph and R.J. Boxer of Rock Haven Island, Lake Rosseau had their big displacement boats re-built. Unfortunately, the changes to Andrews' boat stand only as a credit to Bry's salesmanship; it looked awkward and rode still worse. Today the craft is being changed back by G. Montegu Black of Lake Muskoka. With the weight shifted back the bow rose out of the water and the performance of the new boat became increasingly unstable. No sharp corners in this boat — at any speed!

The Boxer's DIK DON was a newer launch than Andrew's and had a bit more beam. Her bottom was also quite flat at the transom — a feature that was standard in all the later Minett displacement boats. With more bottom aft, in ef-

30. LOU, one of two cruisers built by Minett-Shields in 1930. She is seen here in the yard in Bracebridge nearing completion.

31. Bill Minett in his 27' launch. Built in 1933 for Allan Neilson and still powered with a 200 h.p. Scripps. Bill is Bert Minett's nephew.

fect a hard chine, the DIK DON was a much better modification. The engine was moved back and she was converted to forward drive.

Things slowly fell back into place in 1932-'33 and through the remainder of the decade, anywhere up to a dozen men were employed at the works — though from official records lodged in the Provincial Archives one would surmise that the shop was shut down periodically (of course, what was reported to the government and what actually took place need not necessarily tally).

Bert Minett relinquished any part of the ownership of the business in 1934, but he was certainly around the shop until the war, when he went to work in Hamilton. Through the early 1930s two new lines of boats were introduced; one, 18 feet in length, was a modified John Hacker design. Called a "Class E Racer" in the United States and a "Sports Runabout" by Minett-Shields, it proved very popular when first introduced and this popularity has never waned. A lovely little boat, it resembles nothing so much as a good sports car.

Bob Pridday of Milford Bay, who usually does restoration work, built two of these boats from lines he took from Bob Purves' "FANCY LADY"; one in the 1950's for Nelson Davis of Toronto and Lake Muskoka and one in 1964 for Chester Canning of Toronto and Lake Joseph. Vic Carpenter has only recently built a replica of this model for Bob Russell of Dixon Bay, Lake Joseph and Toronto. As only six were built, they are much sought after.

A slightly larger and similarly-styled boat was introduced about the same time. Four of these 21-foot forward drive models were built, and perhaps the best-known of these today is that owned by our Lieutenant Governor, the Rt. Honourable John B. Aird.

32. Detail of the SEA HORSE, 35', 1928. Owned for years by the Gaby family, her current owner is John Blair of Port Sandfield and Toronto.

33. RADIO II, 21', 1934. Built for R.A. Shields (Bryson's uncle) she is currently owned by David Pardoe of Lake Joseph and New York.

34. BLACK KNIGHT, 18', 1934. Built for Harley Neilson and owned today by Tim Chisholm.

Sometime in 1935, Minett-Shields became the Canadian associates of the Ventnor Boat Works Inc. They held all rights to build special custom craft to the designs of Mr. Adolph Apel — who was among the best known men in racing boat design. The 135-cubic-inch class was created by the American Power Boat Association in 1931 and the 225-cubic-inch class was introduced in 1934. Within two years, all new records established in these two classes were made by Ventnor boats exclusively. In 1936, a Minett-Shields-built "Ventnor", MISS QUEBEC, won the World's Championship at the Canadian National Exhibition and the DELTA, built for Gordon Adamson of Lake of Bays, was raced by her owner at the C.N.E. and won in 1937.

Among the first three-point Ventnor boats built at Minett-Shields in the winter of 1936-'37, were the SHADOW II, built for Chas Wheaton and MISS QUEBEC III for Jack McGuinness. Both of these young men were active in the racing circuit, supported and encouraged by Bryson Shields. The spring of 1938 saw Bryson writing Jack McGuinness at university in New Brunswick, telling him that Charles would go to England to compete for the Duke of York's Race if he would go. At the same time, Bryson wrote Charles saying Jack would go if he would. They both accepted, and Minett-Shields ended up with two of their boats in an international race — where they performed very creditably — with lots of attendant publicity!

Earl Barnes designed a few boats for Shields in 1935-'36. One was a 21-foot runabout, somewhat similar to the 18-footers that had been built a couple of years earlier. Built for Miss Marjorie Balm it is now called OSPREY III and is owned by Ian Gray of Port Cockburn and Port Credit. One other boat was built for Harold Balm, Marjorie's brother: the CAPRICE III. She is a 26-foot streamlined launch with a torpedo stern that was taken to the New York Boat Show in 1936.

35. *A widely used advertisement from 1936.*

36. *MISS QUEBECS.*

37. *DELTA.*

38 - 42. A beautiful 24' forward drive launch built for Fred Burgess in 1934. She was destroyed by fire at the end of her first season.

She is owned today by Alf Mortimer of Port Sandfield.

Some other custom work was done before the war. For instance, the WOODMERE for the Hausermans, and the 26-foot REGODA for Richard Boxer. In addition, half a dozen 22-foot utility boats, equipped with sedan tops, were built — but they are not typical of the company's work.

In January, 1940, Douglas Van Patten left Greavette's and joined Minett-Shields. That winter, 14 new boats were built — everything from 16-foot two-seaters to a 27-foot launch. When the war first started there was a rush to place orders for boats, as everyone realized that if they wanted a boat this would be their last chance for some time. The company was fully occupied with war work and worked at capacity for the duration, in conjunction with the Port Carling Boatworks to begin with, and independently at the end.

After the war, the Fulfords sent their cruiser, the MOBY DICK which Minett-Shields had built for them 16 years before, back to Bracebridge to be rehabilitated. She had been used by the R.C.N. during the war and had been roughly handled. The boat was restored, but legal action was taken over the bill that the company presented. Bryson lost the case and this is commonly considered to have been the final straw for Minett-Shields. In November 1948 everyone was laid off.

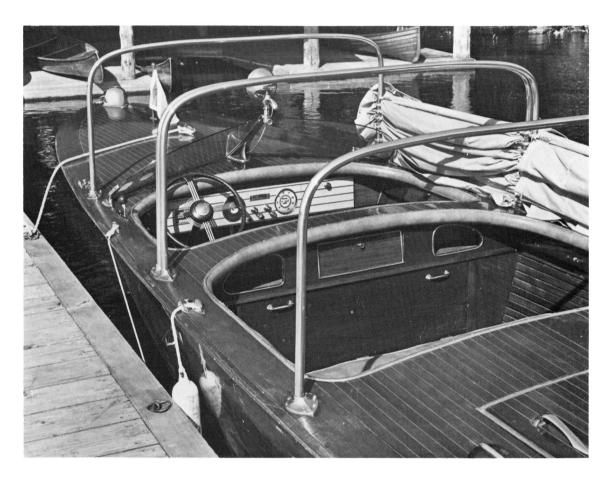

43, 44. WOODMERE, 28', 1939. Built for the Hauserman family, she has been recently taken down to Lake Tahoe in the U.S.A. Mrs. Fred Hauserman and her daughter, Mrs. Rinda Burleigh.

Some work was done on occasion but nothing of significance through 1952. In the following year, the plant was sold and, in 1958, its corporate charter was surrendered. The old shop on the river was demolished in the spring of 1984. Bryson married in 1954 and lived on in Bracebridge until his death in 1975. Bert Minett worked in Hamilton converting Fairmiles after the war and moved back to Bracebridge in the 1950s. He spent most of his time in the summer at his property on Ennis Bay, Lake Muskoka, where his daughter Mrs. Marjorie Johnston and family of Boston visited. He passed away in his 86th year — July 15, 1966, leaving as his monument many fine, graceful boats and a reputation of Master Craftsman.

45. CAPRICE II. Built for Harold Balm and owned today by Alf Mortimer of Port Sandfield (shown at controls.)

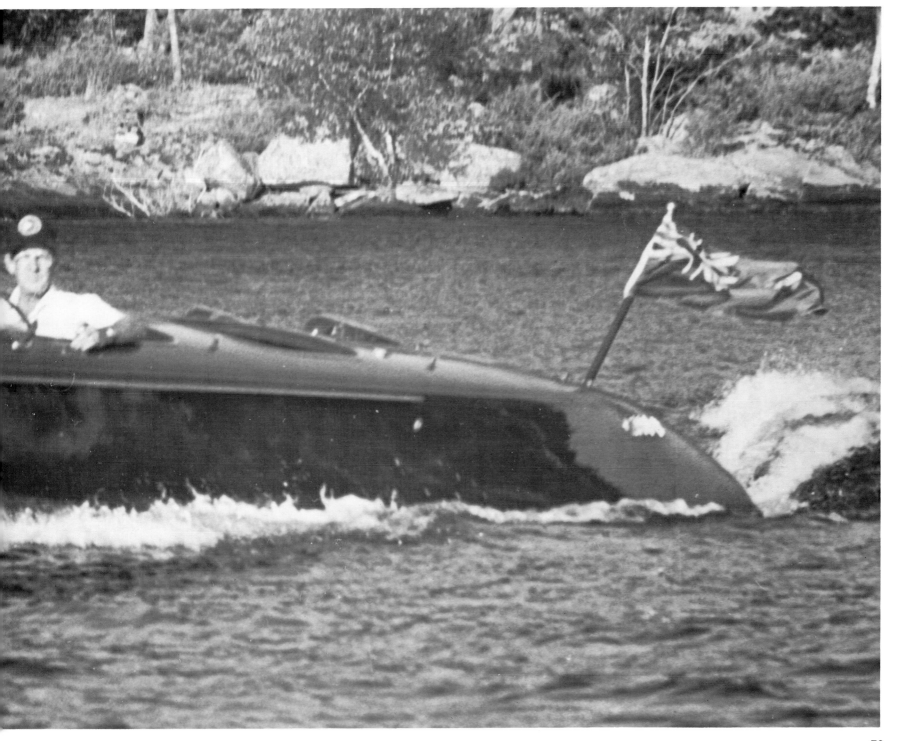

GREAVETTE

In the Muskoka pantheon of boat builders, three names stand above all others: Herb Ditchburn, Bert Minett and Tom Greavette. All were of an age and grew with the industry from the 1890s; each, in his own right, establishing himself within a few short years at the top of his respective field of management, building and sales.

Minett was, of course, an independent, but Ditchburn and Greavette worked hand in glove for more than 30 years before they parted company, leaving Ditchburn as a director and vice-president of sales in 1929. Backed by a very influential and wealthy group of men, Tom Greavette became the key man of a new company called Rainbow Craft Ltd.

The directors and backers of Rainbow Craft were: D.R. Gunn, G. Lefebvre, E. Flavell, T. Greavette, Dr. W.B. Kendall, R. Roy Moodie, R.E. Milburn, S.T. Terry, A.L. Ainsworth and E.A. Wilson. They were all former customers of Ditchburn whom Tom had often courted in the past as the firm's sales manager.

Tom sold the idea of the assembly line principle to his backers, an idea already being used in the U.S.A. For the assembly line to work, they had to bring out a sawn frame-type hull in which the frames and other pieces could be made up at the bench to an exact pattern. We believe this was the first attempt in Canada to build launches on an assembly line.

The enterprise was incorporated in July 1930 and in late October 1930 it was announced that Rainbow Craft Ltd. planned to erect a plant in Gravenhurst.

This modern factory, to cost $50,000, was to be managed by Tom Greavette and initially employ 35 men. The company, backed with half a

1. Tom Greavette.

2. Dart Design: Ensign 18' Built from 1931-1935.

million dollars, would be establishing its head office and showrooms in Toronto; their slogan: "Waterways are sportaways along the Rainbow trail", reinforced the not-so-subtle connection with Greening's RAINBOWS.

Herb Ditchburn, quite naturally, was incensed to see the name Rainbow exploited in this manner. It had been his firm that had built the famous line and, in due course, the new company changed its tune — and name — to Greavette Boats Limited.

Arrangements had been made between the new company's management and Dart Boats of Toledo, Ohio to build Dart models under license for the Canadian market. Dart had been formed in October of 1928 and went into production in 1929 in a plant built with the capacity to turn out three finished boats a day. In 1932 they closed up. Greavette offered four different stock models: the 18-foot Ensign, the 18-foot Roamer, the 23-foot Mohawk and the 26-foot Comet. These boats remained in production until 1933 in Gravenhurst.

Work started on the new Greavette plant in late November, 1930. Built of brick and steel by Carson and Bennett of Orillia, it was a one-storey structure, designed to accommodate two production lines. Boats would be mass produced — one boat a day to be completed on each line. Five months later, in April 1931, the company started operations with a payroll of more than 40 men, amounting to $1,000 a week. J.W. de Beaubien was the superintendent of works, Major Dyas, of Toronto, the sales manager, and Tom Greavette, general manager. The factory began operating day and night, and it was confidently expected that within a very few years the plant capacity would be several times larger and would be offering employment to 200 to 300 men.

75

3. The "Flash", 18' 1935. Six built to a Hacker design.

4. "Cadet", 18' 1935 Lapstrake.

5. The 23' Dictator built to a Hacker design in 1936.

6. Precursor of the Streamliner. A 24' Hacker built in the mid 30s.

Production targets were achieved but not the sales. The same malaise that killed Ditchburn and very nearly did-in Minett-Shields almost finished Greavette as well. After a few months they shut down and over the next two years only re-opened when enough orders had been taken to warrant it.

No doubt the Depression had a lot to do with their troubles but fortunately Muskoka did not suffer as much as other areas. The hotels felt the pinch but people with cottages and extra cash could see no reason why they should not use their facilities as usual. Sales of more moderately priced boats were reasonably good throughout the period.

The spring of 1933 witnessed a reorganization of the company. In January of that year, the plant was re-opened after a closure that had lasted several months. Tom had successfully sold the last stock and had taken enough orders to keep busy for the ensuing six months. The following month, changes were made in the corporate structure. Mr. Lefebvre left the board and was replaced by E.A. Wilson of Ingersoll and Lake Muskoka, as president. Terry and Ainsworth were also dropped from the board. Corporate policy was changed as well; the board realized at last that, given the current economic climate, there was no future in their plan to mass produce stock boats of the Dart design. They officially announced a shift from stock to the custom trade, and on February 16, 1933 made public an arrangement that they had completed with John L. Hacker. He had agreed to design exclusively in Canada for Greavette Boats Ltd. and furthermore agreed to supervise the building of all custom-built boats from then on. This would appear to have been a coûp of major significance, as up until this time Minett-Shields had used his designs almost exclusively. The first fruit of this deal was launched on June 10th of

Custom Built By Greavette

GREAVETTE FLASH

FOR 1935 Greavette brings to you a line of speedy, safe, beautiful, custom built runabouts incorporating many worthwhile features to improve your boating pleasures. And most important . . . the Greavette 1935 runabouts bring you a new conception of softer riding throughout their speed range.

GREAVETTE FLASH . . . A fast, sports 18-foot runabout, the Greavette Flash seats five. A feature is the cleverly arranged forward cockpit which can be opened or closed at will like the rumble seat of an automobile. Closed, the cockpit hatch matches the decking. Beautiful, like all Greavette boats, and a remarkable level-riding, smooth, quiet running boat.

GREAVETTE FURY

GREAVETTE CUSTOM 23-FOOTER

GREAVETTE FURY . . . The famous Little Miss Canada III, 225 cubic inch class design is added to the custom built line of Greavette boats for 1935 as the GREAVETTE FURY. The performance of this world champion racing craft is proof enough that this model is designed to win races. But not only in racing ability do they excel, for these racing craft carry the mark of Greavette quality—now considered to be the utmost obtainable in pleasure craft.

GREAVETTE CUSTOM 23-FOOTER . . .

At last, a positive non-pounding, fast runabout. The Greavette 23 foot runabout shown, as well as the larger 26 foot runabout, have the riding qualities of a round bottom runabout and the speed of a vee bottom. Clever designing brings this great advancement in pleasure boat performance. These Greavette runabouts are round bottom forward and a special design of vee bottom aft, with a wave collector incorporated in the chine, assuring dryness at all speeds. Speedy, safe, beautiful runabouts.

GREAVETTE BOATS LIMITED — GRAVENHURST

7. *Greavette advertisement run in Canadian Boating in 1935.*

8. *CALUMET III, 19' 1939. Designed by Doug Van Patten.*

9. *Trying out a new hull very early in the season.*

that year. LANGLEY IV, 33 feet long, was built for the Wardwells on Little Lake Joseph, for $7,500. It could achieve a speed of 58 m.p.h.

During the association with John L. Hacker, several good models were designed and built, including four early model streamliners. These are best described by the accompanying pictures. In 1936 Hacker designed a larger streamliner for Fred C. Burgess, Burgess Island, Lake Joseph named the CURLEW. Powered with a V-12 Scripps engine, she is presently owned by D.G. Wilmot, Lake Rosseau and King City. At this same time, Greavettes built a boat similar to the CURLEW for John Stevenson at Beaumaris. Designed by Hacker, she was 34 feet long but without the torpedo stern. Hacker was with Greavettes until 1937.

About this time Douglas Van Patten appeared on the scene. Doug is a well known Naval Architect who has designed boats in both North and South America as well as in Europe. Doug was with Greavettes until 1940 when he left to go to Minett-Shields. Tom Greavette asked Van Patten to design a completely elliptical boat. True, they had a streamlined model designed by John Hacker which they built from 1934 to 1936, but Tom wanted a model with more streamlining. Van Patten produced a design which proved to be a very successful hull and with the exception of the war years, was built until 1966, in lengths 22 to 30 feet.

During the 30s Greavettes experimented with different models. In 1936 Dave Fettes designed a small Vee bottom but we are not sure whether this model was built in any quantity; in the same year they built some lapstrake 20-footers, powered with Buchanan Jr. Four engines. About this time Ditchburns were doing the same thing (perhaps they were both influenced by the success of the Port Carling Boat Works' lapstrakes and thought they would try their hand) but neither of these models were very successful.

*10. A Van Patten Streamliner
owned by R. Corcelli of
Gravenhurst.*

11. CURLEW 34', 1936.

In 1936 Greavette acquired the rights to produce Disappearing Propeller boats from Sam Botting of the Lindsay Disappearing Propeller Boat Company and until 1958 turned out three or four hundreds of these small craft. Through the 30s and 40s they were also supplying E.A. Wilson and son Harold of Ingersoll, with racing boats.

The War years saw them making up parts for Fairmiles which they were building in a plant leased from Sachau in Toronto and in 1941-42-43 Greavettes built boats in Gravenhurst for the Royal Canadian Air Force — three 30-foot Crash Boats and three 40-foot Bomber Range Patrol Boats which were transported by rail to larger waterways.

After the War, Van Patten designed the Sheerliner for customers who wanted a more conventional boat. The Sheerliner was attractive in design but not as elaborate as the Streamliner.

In the late 40s Leonard Barnes designed a 20-foot utility boat and in 1950 Earl Barnes designed a 43-foot, 11-foot beam cruiser which Greavettes built for M. Bertheau of Montreal — The ESPADON, a twin-screw job. Also in 1950, Bert Hawker designed a 15-foot inboard and a 17-foot inboard. John Hacker designed Inboard/Outboard 17-foot and 21-foot semi-vee Clippers in the 1950s too. In this same era Greavettes obtained rights and designs to build Lyman-type lapstrake outboards from the parent company in the U.S.A. These were good running hulls and many were built.

When Tom Greavette died in 1958, his daughter Lorraine and her husband Ron MacNab carried on the business until 1962 when C.H. & J.D. Heintzman of piano fame purchased the firm. Ron stayed on the Board of Directors and managed the business until 1972 when Bruce L. Wilson of Toronto purchased the company.

12, 13. *Bert Hurst driving a 24' Van Patten Sheerliner in 1953. Lorraine Greavette McNab, wearing hat, in middle seat.*

14. *Bert Hurst in a 20', 1949.*

15. *43' x 11' Barnes-designed cruiser, built in 1950.*

Bruce Wilson is not related to the Wilsons of Ingersoll.

In the 60's Greavettes used several of Tom Faul's designs of Lapstrake DeepVee I/O's — 17 to 20 feet with painted hulls and 16-foot and 18-foot mahogany I/O models, Sunflash II and Sunflash III. In the late 60's three 18-foot Fire-Flash were built. These beamy little vee-bottom inboard boats were driven from aft of the engine and also had a forward cockpit. The Hon. John Black Aird owned a FireFlash. At this same time, Greavettes were also building 22-foot twin engine I/O's and others with single engine.

During Bruce Wilson's ownership, six ultra-modern, elegant 22-foot mahogany I/O launches were built from a design by Tom Faul. Bruce also had Currie Fibreglass Products, Bala, lay-up six only 18-foot fibreglass I/O hulls from Greavette's Montique model I/O, 18 feet by 85″ beam. These hulls were then fitted out with mahogany decks, etc. and according to Bruce they turned out very well but were too expensive to manufacture.

Bruce Wilson operated the company in the Gravenhurst building from 1972 until 1978 when he decided the company would do better if they moved to Port Carling, so the Gravenhurst plant was sold in October 1978 to Robson's Marina. The company then purchased property in Port Carling below the Locks, opposite Hanna Park, formerly known as Dan Brown's Swamp. Here they built a very substantial shop where their business was mainly the restoration and refinishing of older boats. After operating for a couple of years, Bruce decided the business was unprofitable and closed the company down.

16. Built from 1958-1963 the 18'
Cadet Outboard was planked in
plywood.

17. 21' Sportsman built in the early
'70s .

18. Oscar Purdy in the 18' Fireflash,
one of three built to designs of J.L.
Hacker, 1965.

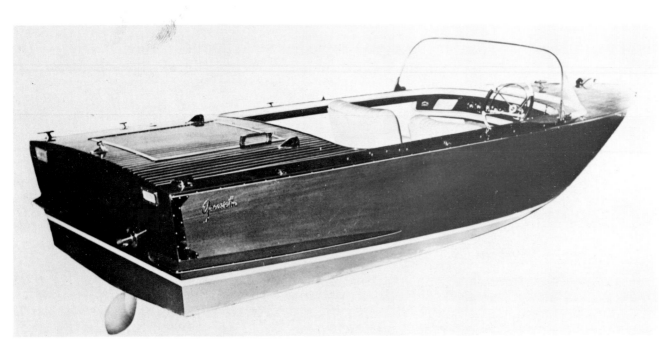

19. The SUNFLASH. This 17'
model was introduced in 1963.

20. A 22' Streamliner built in 1954.
Tim Chisholm, the current owner is
at the controls.

21. A 22' twin engined inboard/outboard built in 1968.

22. Montique, 18' x 85'' designed by Tom Faul. This hull was later made out of fibreglass. Bruce Wilson at the controls.

23. The EXECUTIVE.

Harold Wilson's first boat Little Miss Canada I was a Dart Design. Little Miss Canada II designed by John Hacker and built by Greavettes, won several races in Muskoka. Then in 1933 the 225 Class race was formed North America wide and was to be held at the Canadian National Exhibition in the fall. The Wilsons decided to go for it. Hacker designed a hydroplane for this race; she was built by Greavettes — Little Miss Canada III, powered with a Ford conversion engine. Wilsons won the first World Championship with her.

Boats had to be faster for the 1934 race, so Wilsons had John Hacker design another 225 class boat — Little Miss Canada IV. This hydroplane had a very unusual hull — very streamlined on the decks, almost like a torpedo with two tandem seats for one person in each to compensate for the difference in weight between Harold's 225 lbs. and his co-pilot Lorna's 118 lbs. It was like riding in a kayak. They won again.

The Wilsons raced Little Miss Canada III and IV in various places, not only in Canada but in the U.S.A. at Washington and Baltimore.

Next came Little Miss Canada V but she turned out to be one of those unfortunate things that happen occasionally. She was a beautiful looking boat which ran well but not fast enough, so the Wilsons did not race her.

In 1937 the Wilsons had Douglas Van Patten, who was working at Greavettes at this time, design Little Miss Canada VI. Van Patten's design was quite a startling change as the hull was designed for the engine to be mounted in the aft end with the propeller shaft driven through a Vee drive gear box.

Until this time, they had been using Lycoming engines which produced around 65 m.p.h. Just before the start of World War II Harold and his mechanic Chas. Volker designed a 225 Class

engine which they planned to build in the Wilsons' plant in Ingersoll — Ingersoll Machine and Tool Company — and sell to the racing fraternity. With the start of the War the project was abandoned. When the races were resumed after the War, the engine was disqualified as it had a twin overhead cam; also it was too expensive to manufacture for 225 Class rules. Using this engine, Little Miss Canada VI was very fast — she ran about 78 miles per hour. The engine is now in a museum in Detroit as it was one of a kind.

This ended the Little Miss Canada Series.

Having had their appetite whetted on motor boat racing, the Wilson's set their sights on a bigger challenge. The first MISS CANADA had been purchased from Ditchburns for the Wilsons' pleasure boating on Muskoka Lakes. MISS CANADA II was Harold's first unlimited class hydroplane — designed by John Hacker. She was fast but the hull was not very successful. She had a laminated bottom, planked from narrow strips of wood about 1½″ wide placed vertically and glued together. This construction was intended to make a very strong hull. This it did, but after racing a few times, she leaked like a sieve from every joint from one end to the other. Doug Van Patten worked on her and corrected some of the problems but they finally gave up.

Van Patten was commissioned to design MISS CANADA III. He was told to use the bottom they had developed on MISS CANADA II but the decks would be different. Harold said MISS CANADA III was the best racing boat he had ever driven. In 1939 he won the President's Cup Race in Washington D.C. with MISS CANADA III and President Roosevelt personally presented the Trophy at the White House.

MISS CANADA III was very successful. She won many races and set a North American speed record of 119 m.p.h. She was 24 feet long, powered with a Miller 12 cylinder 1000 H.P. engine at first and later a Rolls Royce Merlin engine 1650 H.P. The transmission was designed and built by Ingersoll Machine and Tool Company of Ingersoll, Canada.

As with so many things in life, you either progress or get out of it. Harold's father Ernie Wilson had been talking to Harry Greening of Hamilton to get a little encouragement to make a Canadian challenge for the Harmsworth Trophy, held by Garwood at that time. Asking Greening for advice to race or not to race was like asking a boy if he wanted some candy! At any rate, the Wilsons decided to reach for the top and again Doug Van Patten was commissioned to design the hull. The design would be the same as MISS CANADA III but increased in size to accommodate the extra weight of a 3000 H.P. Rolls Royce Griffon engine compared to the 1650 H.P. Merlin.

The Wilsons talked to Rolls Royce in England and finally persuaded them to loan the engines. Now MISS CANADA IV — 29 feet long — was ready to roar; she established a record of 173 M.P.H. She was fast but not as good a racing boat as MISS CANADA III. Unfortunately, they had gear box trouble and were unable to complete the race. This ended the era of Harold Wilson's racing career.

Harold was formally inducted into Canada's Sports Hall of Fame August 23rd, 1975, in recognition of his great contribution to Canadian motor boat racing.

24. LITTLE MISS CANADA III at the Golf Club.

25. LITTLE MISS CANADA III and LITTLE MISS CANADA IV at the Muskoka Lakes Association Regatta 1937.

26. Aerial view of the Greavette plant, Gravenhurst.

PORT CARLING

The late Cam Milner said that Port Carling in the 1920s was a "boat builder's town", and that "it always was". While there were a number of people employed in boat building in Bracebridge and a great many more in Gravenhurst, nowhere else in Muskoka was a community more tied to one industry than was Port Carling through the half century 1910 to 1960. Hundreds of men through the years found employment at the "Disappearing", Duke's, Johnston's, Matheson's or the Port Carling Boat Works.

Boat building started soon after Confederation and while the last new boats were built ten years ago, there are still five businesses in the immediate vicinity that still repair, refinish and restore the classic launches. Before we look at the individual firms, it would be profitable to make an overview of the development of the industry in the village, as it is extremely confusing keeping the various characters and firms straight.

As we noted earlier, we are passing over the different people who built scows, steamboats and work boats, simply because we want this work to remain within manageable proportions. The pioneer of the pleasure boat business in Port was undoubtedly W.J. Johnston Sr. Uncle Billy, as he was known to all, or Billy Wagtail for the swallow tail coat he habitually sported, started by building rowboats and canoes for sale and hire. Around 1900, Ditchburn's had established a livery in direct competition with Johnston, and in 1910 John Matheson, a former Johnston employee, put up a shop below the locks building rowboats and gasoline launches. At approximately the same time, Joe Bastien, a boat builder from Hamilton, came up to Muskoka and estab-

lished boat liveries in Port Carling, at The Royal Muskoka Hotel, and at Barnesdale (Lake Joe Station). Early in the century Henry Keyes had built a repair depot above the lock; complete with a marine railway where repairs — both mechanical and structural — could be effected. He did not, however, build or sell boats.

By 1908, A.H. (Bert) Duke went into the business on the Indian River about a third of a mile below the locks. He built custom motor launches. In 1914 there were three boat liveries: Johnston's, Ditchburn's and Bastiens's on the island above the locks; two repair depots; Ditchburn's & Keyes' in the bay above the locks; three builders-Johnston's and Matheson's immediately below the locks; and Bert Duke, a short distance down the Indian River.

The pace quickened during the First World War with the establishment of the Disappearing Propeller Boat Company. It built a large, three-storey factory below the locks, behind the Presbyterian Church, and employed several dozen men. Keyes' shop was bought by Ditchburn as it expanded its depot in Port Carling, and in 1924 C.J. (Charlie) Duke went into partnership with Ernie Greavette who had taken over the old Matheson Shop below the locks in 1923 — while Bert Duke (Charlie's older brother) folded and moved to Toronto.

Perhaps we should take a snap shot of the village in 1926. At that time, the situation had pretty well settled down and the scene was set that was to remain fundamentally unchanged for decades to come. In 1926, Charles J. Duke bought out his partner Ernest Greavette and established the Duke Boat Works — which still is in business under the name Duke Marine Services Ltd. (even though the Duke family retains no part of the business).

The Port Carling Boat Works had been established the year before and is now owned by a former employee, Hugh MacLennan. It is known as

Hugh MacLennan & Sons Ltd. The Disappearing Propeller Boat Co. Ltd. had gone into liquidation in 1924 but was to operate until 1927 in Port Carling. John Matheson was about to get into business again — this time in a boathouse above the locks in the bay north of Whiting's, where he worked until 1940, passing on in 1942.

W.J. Johnston Jr. (Young Billy) was to go into business on his own in 1929 below the locks on the site of the Dispro factory, and work there until he retired shortly before his death in 1956.

In total, the various men and firms in Port Carling turned out something close to two thousand motor boats, excluding war work, from 16 to 30 feet in length, from 1904 to 1968. This is a record that we doubt can be equalled by many small villages in Canada. As Hughie MacLennan says: "the boats may not have carried the prestige names, Ditchburn or Minett-Shields, but they were honest boats — built by dedicated, skilled artisans of first rate materials. The boat builders who worked here were the equal of any anywhere."

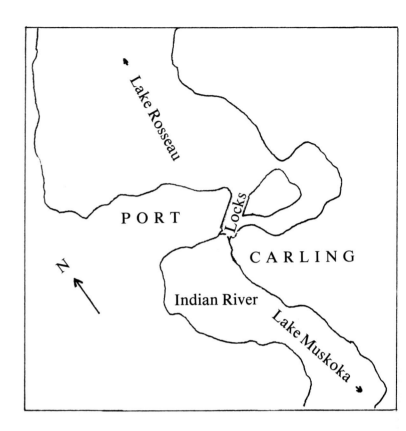

W.J. JOHNSTON SR. & W.J. JOHNSTON JR.

Uncle Billy Wagtail & Young Billy

Whether or not Uncle Billy Johnston was the first boat builder in Muskoka does not really matter — it can't be proved today one way or the other, but he certainly was first in Port Carling. He was among the first generation of builders and in the last quarter of the nineteenth century established a network of boat liveries rivalled only by that of Henry Ditchburn.

The Johnstons were among the earliest pioneering families to open Medora Township, and Uncle Billy's father, Benjamin Hardcastle Johnston, named Port Carling and became its first Post Master in 1869. It was about this time that Uncle Billy graduated from building dugout canoes to building his first rowboat. Over the years he would build another 300 to add to the fleet of boats he maintained for hire in Port Carling, Windermere and Port Sandfield. By 1896 he was also building sailing dinghies, which were probably 14 to 16 feet in length. Helped in the early years by Jack Trouten, he was joined by John Matheson in 1892 and by his nephew William J. Johnston (Young Billy) in 1900.

In the early 1880s Uncle Billy had built a shop just below the locks on the south side of the river, below the site of the recently burned Port Carling Garage. The cribs are still there, and until recently, the old boat-house for the cruiser VEDETTE marked the spot.

It is difficult to determine today when the Johnstons first put their hands to the building of gasoline launches. We do know that Uncle Billy took his nephew into equal partnership in the business in the winter of 1910.

Ferro half planked

1. Port Carling waterfront above the locks showing the boat liveries on the island in 1907. (Pages 91 - 92).

2. Launching boat from Johnston's boatworks c. 1908 just below the locks.

3. Interior view of Johnstons left to right: John Matheson, Young Billy, Uncle Billy, Alf Gage.

Young Billy had been managing the branch in Port Sandfield each summer since 1900 and helping his uncle build boats each winter in Port Carling. John Matheson managed the branch in Windermere during the summer, and like Young Billy, would return to Port Carling in the off season.

Between 1904 and 1910, several launches were built by John Matheson, Young Billy and Alf Gage while in the employ of Billy Sr. The DREADNAUGHT and the FEARNAUGHT were identical sister ships of between 25 to 27 feet in length and equipped with a stationary wooden top covering the open cockpit which had bench seats around the perimeter. Powered by three-cylinder Fero engines located midship, they were used as taxi boats by the Johnstons for one year; the FEARNAUGHT was sold down the lake to the McDivitts, who ran the New Windsor Hotel in Bala. The DREADNAUGHT was run for years by Billy Massey, Uncle Billy's son-in-law. A series of fast launches, the HUMMING BIRDS, were built for J.R.C. Hodgson of Calypso Point Lake Joseph, as well as at least one other launch the FERRO.

In 1910 John Matheson and Billy Johnston Sr. had a serious falling out and Matheson left him to build a shop of his own across the river, below the locks where Duke's is now located. Uncle Billy and his nephew and namesake, Young Billy, stayed in business until 1915 and continued building and renting boats. Young Billy built at least one speed boat, the BLUE-BIRD, with a six-cylinder Pierce Budd engine. This engine was quite a sight, with its row of cylinders each standing separately, clad in copper water jackets. Having direct drive to the propeller, obviously she had to be headed for open water before starting up.

In the summer of 1914, while at Port Sandfield, W. Johnston Jr. with permission from Ed Rogers, improved on a device which W.J. pa-

tented. The device was equipped with a universal joint and an adjustable strut bearing with a skeg underneath so that when a log or rock was hit, the skeg pushed the propeller up into a metal box in the boat. The propeller could also be pulled up into this box by means of a lever to slow down or if the waters were thought to be shallow.

W.J. then built a 16 foot rowboat a plank higher and installed a 2 H.P. Waterman engine in it, attaching the drive-shaft through this metal box. These boats were a big advantage over rowing and about 50 of this model were built in the Port Carling shop.

In 1916 William Jr. formed the Disappearing Propeller Boat Company with J.R. Hodson, giving him 50% interest. They built a fairly large three storey factory south of the original building and a large storage building between the two shops in 1919. In the new shop three different models were built: the WATERFORD, similar to the first but with splash gunwales, the JOHN BULL which was wide — a copy of a government lifeboat and the UNCLE SAM which was longer and leaner with a short front deck.

These boats were well-built little lapstrakes which came along at a good time when people wanted a rest from rowing. The DP's sold for $325 for the Waterford; $375 for the John Bull and $425 for the Uncle Sam.

W.J. Johnston Sr. retired from activity in the boat business at the time the Disappearing Propeller Co. was formed but held considerable stock in the company.

The Dispro Co. employed about forty men; each year they built from 350 to 400 boats which were shipped to half a dozen countries. Later they had Knight Motors of Toronto build their own engines — 3 H.P. Dispro's the same as the Waterman. Wm. Johnston Jr. managed the operation in Port Carling from start to finish but unfortunately the office executive in Toronto became a little greedy, forcing the Company into

4 & 5. Two examples of the style of launch that young Billy built after leaving the Port Carling Boatworks.

liquidation in 1924. Thomas Hodgson of Lindsay, Ontario, a cousin of J.R. Hodgson, bought the assets of the defunct Company in 1926.

After the Dispro Company folded, Wm. Johnston Jr. along with some former employees, formed the Port Carling Boat Works where, as President, he stayed four years. He then acquired the Dispro Factory without the storage building. He reduced the factory building to one storey and built a line of power boats of his own design, operating on a small scale until the second World War. During the war he built rowing Whaler boats for the Navy and after the war, started back on his own line of pleasure boats.

With his uncle Rob Johnston as his first helper, he began building a model very similar to the Port Carling Boat Works launches but later his boats had their own characteristics. He usually built a couple of boats a year, changing into forward drive models in the early 1930's. Billy designed and built a good running hull which was quite fast for its power but then Billy was always somewhat of a speed demon. His boats were not very strong though.

One particular boat he built created a great deal of interest and still does. She was the SCHERZO designed by Hacker and built for Harry Greening, now owned by George Wycoff of Beaumaris. SCHERZO is a 20-foot lapstrake both bottom and topsides, with one step. She has a fairly long stern deck and a one seat cockpit with long front deck. SCHERZO was built very light with a thin veneer deck covered with canvas, and was originally powered with a Buchanan "souped up" 6 cyl. engine.

Billy was a wood-worker and usually worked with one man. Over the years different men spent some time with him but during the War he had several on his staff. He retired from business in 1956 at the age of 75 and died in 1968 after a lifetime in the boating industry.

6. *W.J. Johnston trying out one of his boats above the locks.*

7. *The SCHERZO, Harry Greening at the wheel.*

THE PORT CARLING BOAT WORKS

After the collapse of the Disappearing Propeller Company in 1924, Wm. Johnston Jr. with former employees Cameron and Douglas Milner, Harold Cooper and Chas. J. McCulley, formed a limited company — The Port Carling Boat Works. Hal Clerk and Bud Harris who had been at the Dispro, also went with them but were not shareholders. R.A. Shields and Dr. R.J. Hutchison were the financiers. This group built a factory above the locks further down from the Government Wharf on the north side, in 1925. This building is now owned by Hugh MacLennan & Sons.

In order to get around the patent of the Dispro Device, Wm. Johnston Jr. set up shop in the upper storey of the Port Carling Garage, which had originally been built for a store by W.J. Johnston Sr. Here he laid out and built a hull which was named the Johnston Special. This hull was similar to the Dispro but with a high rise in the keel toward the stern. A wooden shaft log was installed on the outside of the boat, on which a bearing and stuffing box were attached to support the shaft. The shaft was so located through the shaft log that about one third of the propeller was above water when she was sitting at rest but when underway with people onboard, she settled down on the stern and gave the propeller a good grip in the water, at the same time offering some protection to the propeller. The accompanying picture tells it all.

A 1 cylinder 4 cycle engine named Firefly, which was brought out by F.L. Buchanan of Orillia, was installed. It had one advantage over the Dispro in that it had a reverse gear which made the boat more manoeuverable. However, this boat was not a best seller as the "bugs"

1. Port Carling c. 1960. The Boatworks are on the waterfront lower right.

2, 3. The Johnston Special.

The Johnston Special

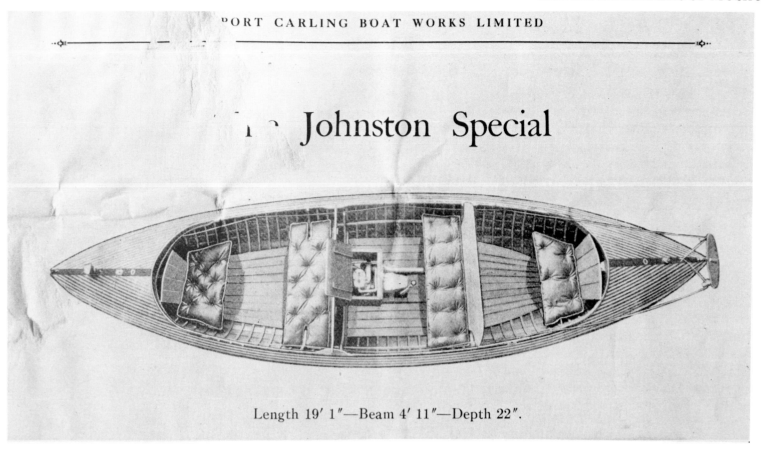

Length 19′ 1″—Beam 4′ 11″—Depth 22″.

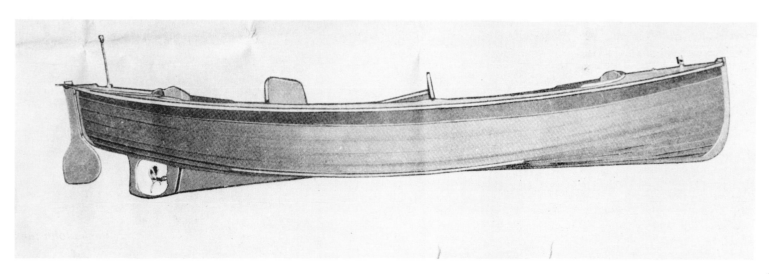

hadn't been eliminated from the new engine and the hull did not ride well. It doesn't appear the Johnston Special was built for more than one year, with only a dozen or so produced.

While Johnston was getting out this boat, Harold Cooper, Hal Clerk, Chas. McCulley and John Dixon as their "gofor" were operating a repair depot in the old Bastien Shop on the Island above the locks to look after their Dispro customers. Douglas Milner was making plans for the new building and Cameron Milner worked in Gravenhurst at Ditchburns, building the WHIPPET for Ewart McLaughlin.

During the time Johnston was with the firm, he did all the designing. Doug Milner planked and Bud Harris nailed for him. Cam Milner did the finishing with a helper and Johnston looked after getting out the material. In the summer Harold Cooper was in charge of the mechanical repairs with Hal Clerk and Cam Milner did the installations. Cooper and Clerk were in the varnish room with Reg Stephen during the winter.

From the start of their operation they built a line of cedar lapstrake outboards and 14 and 16-foot rowboats. In one day Cam Milner would make ten oars ready to sand. Their next venture was a 17-foot centre-drive, round bilge cedar lapstrake with a square transom. She had a stern seat and a driver's seat aft of the engine as well as a forward cockpit. The decks were installed with wide mahogany boards flush-screwed to the deck beams. These boats were fitted out with Universal 4 cylinder 15 H.P. engines. The hulls were designed with a decidedly abrupt lift in the keel from about 8 ft. to the stern — a very unusual shape. At least one of these boats, built in 1928, is around today and is presently being restored by Rob Haggar Wooden Boats for Ron Hill. Almost at this same time, the Boat Works brought out similar models to 22 feet as well as building two smoothskin boats, one for R.A. Shields and the other for Dr. Hutchison.

PORT CARLING BOAT WORKS LIMITED

The Sea Bird

4. *An illustration of the early
SeaBird.*

5. *Dr. Hutchison's smoothskin
SeaBird c.1929.*

6. *SAMMY, c. 1930.*

R.A. Shields named the first boat SEA BIRD and from then on Port Carling Boat Works' launches were known as SeaBirds. In fact, as often as not, many people referred to the company as SeaBird. Later on each new model was named after a bird — Tern, Loon, Hawk etc.

F.L. Buchanan Co. Ltd. of Orillia were building a 4 cylinder 4 cycle 25-30 H.P. and a 6 cylinder 25-40 H.P. for which they used Continental Engine Blocks. They built their own reverse gear and did all their own casting of parts to convert the engines for marine use. It seems R.A. Shields was the white knight behind Buchanans as well as the Port Carling Boat Works so it would be natural for him to push the product in which he had a financial interest. A good many SeaBirds had Buchanan engines.

Whether or not there were too many "Chiefs", Wm. J. Johnston Jr. withdrew from the firm in 1929 after four years of operation. After Wm. J. Jr. left, R.A. Shields became President and C.J. (Chas.) McCulley retained the job of Secretary-Treasurer.

The Milner boys were very aggressive, energetic workmen — both having completed Public School when twelve years old. We believe a great deal of the success of Dispro and the Port Carling Boat Works can be credited to their ability.

In 1931 the Company changed over from centre-drive boats to forward drive and Buchanans changed to using Hercules cylinder blocks. The engines were smaller with higher compression. The 45 H.P. engine was a "Jr. Four" and eventually got up to 57 H.P.; the "Rocket" was 85 H.P. and the early 95 H.P. was the "Meteor" later boosted to 105 H.P.

An advertisement in Canadian Homes & Gardens magazine, dated May 1931, shows a 20-foot lapstrake forward drive or centre-drive, powered with a Buchanan 4 cylinder 20-30 H.P.

7. *Cam Milner, 1941.*

8. *Doug Milner, 1941.*

9, 10. *Top picture: framed smoothskin hard chine model. Topsides planking screwed and plugged. Lower picture: lapstrake hull flush nailed.*

11. *A very popular model, built from the mid 1930s on. Came with or without the sedan top. This 18' hull was powered typically with a 4 cylinder 20-30 H.P. Buchanan.*

12. *Same as 11 but with a navy top. Chas. McCulley is at wheel.*

engine for $1,450.00; Smoothskin $1,850.00 both fully equipped, which would be a pretty good price for the times.

On October 27th, 1931, the Port Carling Boat Works' plant completely burned down, preceeding by one night the destruction of the entire business section on the northwest side of the bridge. Like most of the other businesses, the Boat Works immediately started to re-build a bigger and better building. By Spring, most of the business section of Port Carling was completed and the Boat Works too was back in business — right in the midst of the Depression!

Since they were building boats in the lower price range, they were soon very busy and by this time had enlarged their staff considerably. Stan McNab had been selling their boats on Georgian Bay and it was clear there was a good potential in that area, so a small marina was purchased at Honey Harbour. Doug Milner headed up the operation the first summer in 1935 and Cam Milner carried on in the summers until the start of the War.

In 1934 they built a 17-foot cedar planked mahogany deck lapstrake, forward drive, round bilge boat powered with a Buchanan Jr. Four. This model had the driver's seat forward of the engine and a stern seat aft. The engine was decked over with one single hatch and two small seats, one on either side of the engine. These were often referred to as Mother-in-Law seats. This model sold for $1,095.00 and as an inducement to buy, in some cases, free storage was offered for the first year.

During 1935, Cam made a wooden model of a ''cigar boat'' from which the Boat Works built two boats — one for Reg Boxer, powered with a straight eight Buchanan or Gray 100 H.P. engine.

In the 30's they changed their models from round bilge to Vee bottoms. The first was a reverse lapstrake on the bottom (the opposite to a

rowboat). Cam thought this would make the boats more spritely. However, they were changed back to standard lap and then to conventional double skin. Later their boats had single planked bottoms using ⅝″ cedar screwed to frames and copper rivetted to ribs. Their topsides were smoothskin and a good many were flush-nailed with copper nails. However, the Boat Works' better line of launches were screwed and plugged.

Then came the War. They had six 20-foot forward drive boats on hand at the start of the War which the Air Force purchased but the aluminum stems had to be removed and wooden stems installed to withstand salt water. They also had to build a small cabin on the aft end and a canvas cover protection over the driver's seat. These launches were powered with a Buchanan Jr. Four engine and the first two boats were fitted out with regular chrome fittings but the remainder had brass.

Port Carling Boat Works had a contract to build 25-foot motor cutters and later obtained a contract in partnership with Minett & Shields of Bracebridge, to build Fairmiles. Their operation in Port Carling was largely making up parts for Fairmiles. They were fortunate they had obtained the property at Honey Harbour on Georgian Bay prior to this date, as it made an ideal opening to the Great Lakes. Here they built a factory and several of their men from Port Carling worked at this location. After the War, the Company disbanded. Cam Milner took over the Honey Harbour plant; Douglas Milner went into Real Estate and property development and C.J. McCulley carried on the Port Carling operation with the same type of business as pre-war. Quite a number of the old hands stayed with McCulley. Leone McCulley had been in the office with her father for several years while Douglas McCulley, Chas' son, had grown up with the Company.

13. A 20' launch with a very high crown built 1936.

14. Harold Cooper in 26' launch built C. 1938.

15. left to right: (upstairs) Tup Amey, Pete Anderson, Jack Nicholson, Russel Eaton. (ground level) Bud Harris, Anthony Gonneau, Eric Stephen.

The family operated the Port Carling Boat Works until 1958 at which time they sold to Bruce Cordick. Manufacturing ceased when McCulley sold out but Cordick brought in some skelton Grady-Whyte hulls for fitting out.

C.J. stayed with the new owner for the first summer. Grant Slater managed the business for Cordick until it was sold to Hugh MacLennan & Sons in 1965. Hugh Sr. had been a mechanic with the Boat Works since 1937. Hugh MacLennan & Sons is still operating with service work and restorations.

Douglas Milner passed away in Florida in 1976.

Cameron Milner passed away in Midland in 1978.

Chas. J. McCulley, who is rubbing 90, spends most of the year in Florida but comes to Muskoka for the summer.

16. Doug McCulley in a 20', vee bottom — one of the last models.

17, 18. At the boatshow 1956. (left to right) Tom Greavette, Sam Shepherd, Charlie McCulley.

109

JOHN MATHESON

John Matheson's boat building career in Port Carling spanned half a century. Born in Scotland to a boat building family, he ran away to sea when he was 12 years old, shipping out in a square-rigger that had a run between Scotland and Russia carrying salt herring.

By 1884 Matheson had immigrated to Canada and started working for Harry Hodgson, a well-known boat builder located at the foot of York Street in Toronto (Today's Toronto harbour has been totally rearranged — the Harbour Commission has filled in the old waterfront — but at that time Hodgson's boathouse was found where Union Station is now located).

In 1890 John left Hodgson to come to Muskoka to build a couple of boats for the Toltons who farmed near Minett. Tolton was also a builder and he had a contract with Mr. John Herbert Mason (a founder and principal of the Canada Permanent) to build a cottage on Chief's Island in Lake Joseph. Matheson and his wife spent the winter of 1890/'91 on the island doing the finishing work (the cottage was very large; one of the first and earliest 'grand' cottages to be built in Muskoka). They very nearly starved to death and if it had not been for a helpful neighbor — Mr. George Croucher of Craigie Lea — our boat builder's story might well have ended here! It is believed that Matheson went to work for W.J. Johnston of Port Carling in 1892, but there is a single reference found to a "John Matheson boat building" in an 1894 Toronto directory to suggest that he might have tried to set himself up in business independently. We do know that in 1896 he helped Johnston build a sailing dinghy for the Schriebers, the "Freija". In the winters from here on he built boats with Johnston and managed Johnston's livery in Windermere during the summers.

John Matheson was an excellent sailor as well as an expert wood-worker. He taught John Eaton, the Schriebers, Dr. Hinks, the Whittemores, among others, how to sail. It is thought today that he taught the Johnstons how to build sailboats as well as many of the finer points of boat building in general.

In 1910 he had a falling out with Uncle Billy Johnston. This was no minor tiff, but a disagreement of the scale that can only be found between two strong-minded men in a small town; they did not talk to each other for one and one-half years. Matheson set up a shop of his own directly across the river from Johnston, about sixty yards away, and went into business on his own building rowboats and launches. Here he worked with one helper, and a good number of the men who were to shine in the business in later years got a start with him. Matheson's workers universally praised him as a fine craftsman and felt anything you learned from John Matheson you never forgot. (Mind you, you learned the hard way).

John never used power tools — everything was done by hand in the early years. Even though he built at least one launch and 25 rowboats every winter, all the materials were got out by hand. Cam Milner who started working for Matheson in 1912 at the age of thirteen, remembered well they purchased white oak in the rough. His job was to hand saw the boards to make ribs for the boats at wages of $5.00 per week. John's one concession by 1912 was a generator to provide electric light in the shop. Bob Perrier, a mechanic who worked for Matheson many summers, had rigged up the generator powered by a one-lung stationary engine. The electric lights would pulsate with the stroke of the engine — bright one second — dim the next, but at least they had electric lights, which was something in Port Carling at that time.

1. *Port Carling below the locks before 1920.*

2. *CRUSADER, 35' built 1911-1912 for George Milburn. She was powered with a 4 cylinder Buffalo engine.*

Between 1910 and 1923, before Matheson sold out the old Shop below the Locks, he built several boats to 32 feet in length. One was the BIG BOY for W.L. Mellon at Squirrel Island, Beaumaris and another the DUQUESNE for Mrs. James Brown, also of Beaumaris. Later owned by the Judds at Rest Harbor and re-named the SEA QUEEN, she was sold to John C. Gray for conversion to a small steam yacht. The conversion was not very successful so she was discarded. Other boats were the DESIRÉ, a varnished cedar or cypress hull, built for the Whittemores, powered with a 4-cycle 20 H.P. Kermath, the CRUSADER for George Milburn, and in 1922 a 26-footer for Dr. C. Hincks. Livery boats were built for Harper Walker and George Riley, both of Milford Bay. Later during this period, Matheson built some 20 foot boats which were painted white and powered with a Universal 4 cylinder 4-cycle engine, equipped with a rear hand-starter. These engines were a big improvement over early types. Mr. Coyne who had a cottage near the mouth of the river owned one, as did Allan Blachford of Mazengah Island.

The last boat built in the old shop was the DOLLY VARDEN presently owned by Matheson's grandson, John Dixon. Built for George Milburn for a fishing boat, she looked more like a sailboat than a launch. She is 20 ft. in length, very low freeboard with very wide covering board around the cockpit; the decks are canvas covered. The engine which is boxed over, is controlled from the stern seat. She was originally fitted with a Kitchen Rudder.

It is almost certain that Matheson took in a 32-foot hull built in 1922 by McNeil & Norris of Bala, to finish. She was later sold by McNeil & Norris to A. Bickmore at Pleasant View Hotel, Lake Muskoka. PLEASANTVIEW is still around the Lakes.

3. SNIPE, built for Mr. Hallock, Duquesne Island before 1918.

4. DUQUESNE, later called the SEA QUEEN.

5. MISSKOKA, built in 1921. She was 30' x 8', vee bottom, powered by a 225 H.P. Kermath.

After Matheson sold his shop below the locks to Ernie Greavette in 1923, he tried retirement for a few years but did not find it to his liking. Deciding to go back into boat building, he purchased a large boathouse that Joe Ruddy had bought from Sir John Eaton at Kawandag, Rosseau, and moved to Port Carling on two large scows belonging to the Tannery in Bracebridge. The building was 60 ft. × 26 ft. wide, two full storeys plus attic. It was moved onto cribs on property owned by Ruddy above the Locks, on the south-west corner of the bay. Ruddy had rented the building to Dr. Cooper for a boathouse and possibly living accommodation upstairs, but Dr. Cooper died before he occupied the building so in 1927 Matheson bought it from Ruddy to use for his Shop. Here he built some very fine boats, both centre and forward drive.

In 1930 Matheson built a 26-foot centre-drive for Edwin Milburn who had an island at Mortimer's Point. She was a mahogany job in typical Matheson style. Anyone familiar with Matheson boats would recognize TIPTOES anywhere. She is still on the Lakes. The MISS-KOKA was built in 1932 for George Milburn. She was a 30 footer with an 8 ft. beam, a forward drive mahogany V-bottom launch powered with a 225 H.P. Kermath overhead camshaft engine. MISSKOKA had a large cockpit forward of the engine. John Dixon thought she might have been designed by Milburn but we think the bottom was most likely designed by John Hacker or another naval architect with Milburn doing the arrangement plan (interior, deck, etc.). This boat was last seen on Lake Simcoe some twenty years ago.

Matheson always turned his boats over to finish, caulk and paint the bottom. MISSKOKA was too large to do this, so he and Chas (Tup) Amey turned her up on the chine, finishing one side, then the other. Matheson soaked his transoms for a couple of days before steaming and fitting. Tup remembers chopping a hole in the ice in front of the shop, tying a cord to the wide board and putting it into the water. Later they re-cut the hole in the ice to retrieve it to steam and fit.

Matheson's last two launches were 24-foot, 6 ft. beam forward drive mahogany boats built in 1934 — one going to Georgian Bay and the other to Dr. A.D.T. Purdy who has a cottage up the shore from Windermere. Apparently he built and repaired outboards and rowboats from '34 on and had a partly built rowboat on the stocks when he died. Two fine examples of his craftsmanship are on permanent display in the Port Carling Pioneer Musuem — a rowboat and an outboard. His business gradually slowed down to a stop in 1940.

It seems John couldn't sit still. His neighbour Alf Johnston used to say that John had a pile of bricks in his basement which he would move around when he didn't have anything else to do. After he stopped building boats he kept himself busy with a small launch which he parked at the government wharf, jitneying people to their cottages or sightseeing.

As mentioned earlier, John usually worked with one man and although there may have been others, Cam Milner, Tup (Chas) Amey, Vernon Harris and Eric Stephen were the main men who got a good start in the craft while working in Matheson's Shop. His grandson John Dixon worked with him some winters in the early '30s.

John Matheson built a number of launches and left a reputation among his peers as an excellent builder. He died in Port Carling in 1942 at age seventy-nine.

6. NENONE, built 1922, 25' present owner Walter K. Donaldson, Tobin's Island

7. Dr. Purdy in his 24' x 6' launch built in 1934.

ALBERT H. DUKE

A.H. DUKE

In addition to the Johnstons and John Matheson, the Dukes were involved in boat building in Port Carling before the First World War. C.T. Duke was a cabinet-maker from Toronto who came to Muskoka in 1896 to build a cottage for the Grand family of Toronto (Grand & Toy) on Grandview Island. He stayed in the contracting business and did a great deal of work in the Beaumaris area. Five of his sons: Albert, Charles, Rupert, Arthur and Ernest (Toby) were involved in boat building.

The eldest son, Albert H. (Bert), set up business in Port Carling in the early 1900s, building furniture in a shop located about half way between the locks and Hanna Park on the Indian River. The furniture he built there is described as 'mission type' — rather heavy looking oak work with square lines. There are still quite a few pieces of it in the Beaumaris area where Bert's father C.T. 'pushed it'. Bert's brother Charlie worked with him on and off and together they built a boat in 1910: the SYNEKEGO, for Wm. Lees of Hamilton. That summer, when Charlie and Bert parted company, 12-year-old Cameron Milner was hired by Bert as a helper. Among the more interesting of Cam's chores was to get under the planked hull holding a candle so that Bert could check for light and the tightness of his seams!

While Bert continued building furniture for a while, it was as a launch-builder that he is best remembered. He produced a number of good-sized mahogany launches until 1921 or 1922, when he folded up and returned to Toronto; there he built "Sea Swift" boats in partnership with Wm. Ogilvie for a year or two before going to work for Heintzman's, building pianos.

As Bert's son Allan Duke remembers it, his father was the first person to put an aluminum stem on a boat. The stem had a rabbet in it that was drilled and tapped to receive machine screws to take the planking. Cam Milner and George Leask were among those who worked for Bert and the general consensus was that while he was as fine a craftsman and mechanic as anyone around he was "cranky as hell".

In a sense Bert worked himself into bankruptcy; he would build a couple of boats and then stop to expand his shop. He did this for several years until he simply ran out of steam — and money. Apparently the ubiquitous R.A. (Alex) Shields from New York City and Glencoe Heights on Lake Joseph had played some role in financing him; after he failed, his shop came into Shield's possession, and from there it went to Port Carling Boat Works (which Mr. Shields also helped to back). They used it for storage.

One of the anecdotes still popular around Port Carling involves Bert Duke and Bill Croucher. In 1913 or 1914 Bert had finished a boat and launched her. She was moored below the shop and had not yet taken-up so there was a lot of water in the bilges. Bill Croucher was installing the engine when he saw a school of minnows. He took a pail, dipped them up, and dumped them into the bottom of the boat. Bert came down from the shop and saw one minnow, then a second and a third. Finally he asked the obvious, "Where did they come from?" Bill Croucher snapped back, "Through the God damn cracks — how else do you expect!"

Among Bert's boats were the GRANDVIEW for the Grands, the RESOLUTE for Col. Royce, boats for Mr. Ham and Mr. Jenckes, two identical launches for the Millers of Beaumaris, and his last, a vee-bottom for Martin Gardner of Port Sandfield (now owned by Wm. Balfour of Ancaster and Star Island, Lake Joseph).

1. SYNEKEGO, built 1910.

2. OSPREY I, built 1917. Owner W.T. Gray at wheel.

3. JAY CEE GEE, built around 1920 for John C. Gardner of Toronto and Port Sandfield.

DUKE BOATS

Duke Boats is the sole active survivor of all the boat works that flourished in the 1920s and 1930s on the Muskoka Lakes. Although the management and ownership of the business passed from family hands in 1977, it is still operated under the name Duke Marine Services and remains primarily concerned with wooden boats, their restoration and maintenance. Between its reorganization in 1926 and 1968 (the year the last launch was built) just less than 400 boats were built, excluding war work, rowboats and canoes.

The founder of the business was C.J. (Charlie) Duke. Charlie began his boat building career when a boy by making a dugout canoe; however, he got his start as a craftsman by working with his father who was in the business of constructing cottages around the lakes. Charlie was soon working in construction on his own and when he was twenty-three years old, he tendered and got the contract to build the original Town Hall in Port Carling in 1905.

In 1910, while in partnership with his brother Bert, they built the boat SYNOKEGO for Wm. Lees of Hamilton. How long he was with Bert is unknown. Then in 1916, in a shed in his back yard on Bailey Street, he built a 30-footer SPEEDAWAY which he used for livery work for a short time. He worked at Ditchburn's in Gravenhurst for awhile, then at the Disappearing Propeller Boat, Port Carling, finishing Dispros.

Charlie went into partnership with Ernie Greavette in 1924 under the name Duke & Greavette. Ernie had worked in Port Carling for some years as mechanic at the Ditchburn repair shop, with Max Croucher as helper. Max and his brother Don moved to Toronto where they spent many years at the Royal Canadian Yacht Club until retirement. Ernie next worked as a planker

1. C.J. (Charlie) Duke, c. 1932.

2. SPEEDAWAY, 30', 1916. She was built by Charlie in Port Carling in his backyard to use as livery boat.

119

at the Dispro. In June 1923 Ernie purchased John Matheson's Shop below the Locks and took in Garnet Massey as partner for one or two summers, doing mechanical repairs to boats.

The partnership which Charlie and Ernie formed in November 1924 did not last very long; in December 1926 it was dissolved, with Duke taking over the Shop and forming Duke Motor Service and Greavette returning to Gravenhurst.

Claude Duke, Charlie's older son, had been working for Ernie Greavette in the summer of 1924 before C.J. came into the picture, and he continued with his father. Son Aud started two years later in 1928 and the brothers formed a formal partnership with their father in the early 30's. Later on their sister Alva worked in the office.

Duke and Greavette's idea had been to establish a network of service centres around the Lakes but it was hard enough to operate one shop due to lack of money and skilled personnel. Their idea was about thirty years ahead of time. Duke and Greavette started off building a few 20-foot displacement launches powered with 15 H.P. and 45 H.P. universal engines, and as many rowboats as they could manage through the winter months. This schedule was continued after the company became Duke Motor Service.

A fourteen foot rowboat with one pair of spoon oars, rudder included, sold for $65 and the sixteen footer for $75. Fifty years later, the last Duke rowboat carried a pricetag of $850 — without oars! If you could get one built today, it would cost about $1500.

Along with the 20-footers Dukes later built boats to 25 ft. The 25-footers were powered with 50 H.P. Kermath engines — big, heavy, slow-turning, vibrating, reliable engines. Mr. Allan Blachford of Mazengah Island was one of the proud owners of these first mahogany hulls, and among others who had the 20-footers were the Vaughans of Linger Longer, Lake Rosseau, the

*3, 4. Joe Vaughan's 21'
displacement launch built c. 1927,
powered by a Universal Super Four.*

Marshes of Belle Isle, Lake Muskoka and the Clause family of Black Forest, Lake Joseph. In 1928, Edwin Mills had Dukes build a 21-ft. mahogany launch, powered with a 25-30 H.P. Buchanan, as a wedding present for his sister Lillian. Then came the tail end of the twenties when everything was roaring. In addition to production work during this period, Duke built two 30-footers — one for W.S. Hodgens of Dominion Securities and the other for H.R. Douglas of the Mail & Empire. The Hodgens' boat is still around, now owned by the Reid family of Milford Manor and the other had its demise when the Douglas boathouse burned.

After the 30-footers, Dukes built two 27-footers to order; one for W.S. Hodgens and the other for Murray Fleming, son-in-law of E.R. Wood of Mazengah Island. These boats still had round bilge hulls but were more sporty looking. Mr. Hodgens' boat was powered with a Scripps 135 H.P. engine. She had a long stern deck, a short cockpit and a long front deck with a forward cockpit seating two.

Although the second order was cancelled during construction, the boat was completed (on spec) and sold to Wm. T. Gray, Croft of Dounie, Lake Joseph who named her OSPREY II. This hull was built as a standard centre-drive boat (engine forward of the cockpit) but when the time came to detail the arrangement plan, she was set out for forward drive.

She was used this way for several years until John C. Gray became the owner and had her changed back to a centre-drive, which made her a much better riding boat. In designing a boat for centre-drive there is usually a fair little lift in the keel towards the transom so that when the boat is at rest, the transom is barely in the water but when she gets under way, she comes down on the aft part of the bottom, raising the bow. When this design is applied to a forward drive hull (with the engine aft of midships) the boat rises

5. SNEGDOH II, 30', 1930. Built for H.S. Hodgens and owned today by the Reids of Milford Manor. Bud Reid is at the wheel.

6. OSPREY II, 27', 1930. Bill Gray at the wheel.

7. Claude Duke in 21' launch, one of the first foward drive boats they built.

too much in the bow. Round bilge boats are designed to go through the water not over it as Vee Bottoms do and are much smoother riding than a Vee Bottom.

OSPREY II has a rather interesting history. When fire broke out in Hanna's store in Port Carling on 31 October 1931, it was soon evident that the whole wooden village centre would be destroyed. In an effort to salvage everything possible, a crew of men on the second floor of Duke's shop pushed new hulls and those under repair over the well and let them drop into the open water in the slip 10 feet below — where they landed upright. A dramatic launching indeed! One of these boats was the OSPREY II and another a 28-foot Ditchburn belonging to J.S. Douglas of Highlands, Lake Rosseau.

The year before the Dukes lost their Shop, their storage facility, the old Dispro warehouse, had been burned by an arsonist. Launches worth more than $100,000 were lost, including all three launches owned by Britton Osler of Windermere. Undeterred by these setbacks, the Dukes rebuilt the storage building and shop; both remain in use today.

Charlie did all his designing from wooden half models, but rather than taking the solid piece of wood required to make the model (like everyone else) he would take a thin piece, one-half-inch in thickness and wide enough to represent the width of the model. He glued these together with a piece of wrapping paper between each joint and then carved the built-up piece until he arrived at a satisfactory shape. He would then separate the individual layers and from these lay the lines down full size to make the molds and frames. While it was much easier than trying to caliper the measurements off the whole model, he did not end up with any models to varnish and put on display. Until he passed away in 1954, he designed all the round-bottom boats the Shop built.

8. "Custom" launch, designed by Charlie Duke and built in the mid '30s.

9. CRUSOE, 30', 1952. Built for John Reilly of California and Lake Muskoka and owned today by the Saer family of New Orleans.

In 1933 Dukes were asked by John Stevenson of Beaumaris to build a fishing boat something like a Dispro but wider and with a square stern. She was powered with a Buchanan Baby Four 15 H.P. converted from an Austin car engine. A great deal of interest was shown in this boat which became the prototype of the PLAYMATE and during the next twenty-one years another 150 were built.

In 1934 four Playmates were built using the Baby Four engine; after '34 all Playmates were powered with a Buchanan Midget 25 H.P. using a Hercules block. All other castings were made by Buchanans of Orillia. This centre-drive Playmate was built until 1938 when one forward drive model was built. The hull was a plank higher and all Playmates were built this way from '39 on. They became more "spiffed up" as time went on.

Through 1935 to 1940, Playmates were by far the largest part of Dukes' production but some 22 and 23-foot Custom built Deluxe Smoothskins were made. These were round bilge design, carvel planked to the keel and were decked over with three cockpits, two forward of the engine and one aft. Dukes also built a few 19-footers which were very similar to the Playmate. They were forward drive, powered with a Buchanan Jr. Four 45 H.P. and called "Playmate Deluxe".

In 1940 Dukes brought out their best designed models — 19-footers and 21-footers. These boats were both the same style, one a little larger than the other in all respects. They were Semi Vees. Both had lap bottoms and the 19-footer was built with either smoothskin or lap on the topsides. The 21-footers were smoothskin only. Both had cedar bottoms with mahogany topsides and decks. The 19-footers were powered with 4 cylinder Buchanan 57 H.P. or Gray 4-75 H.P. The 21-footers had Buchanan 6 cylin-

10. Late model Playmate, built from 1939 - 1956.

11. Early Playmate, built from 1935-1938.

der Meteors 95-105 H.P. or Gray 6 cylinder 104-112 H.P. In place of a chine, these models had a thick plank which made them very much the same as a Vee Bottom.

Production of all pleasure boats was cut in 1942 due to War contracts for whalers and 25-foot Motor Cutters powered with Diesel engines.

After the war, the production of Playmates, 19 and 21-footers resumed along with a few special boats. One was a 30-footer mahogany forward drive boat built in 1952 for J.B. Reilly from California and Crusoe Island, Lake Muskoka. She had a stationary sedan top covering three seats forward of the engine. In 1953 the building of Playmates was discontinued.

A set of plans for a 20-foot Vee Bottom hull was purchased in 1952 from John Hacker, N.A. of Detroit. From these plans Dukes built one boat for Walter Ford and another in '53 for Dr. Fielden of Bala. This model was powered with a ChrisCrafft M.B.L. 158 H.P. They were nice little boats with one seat forward of the engine. In 1956 Dukes stretched the plan out to 22 ft. and built two more — one for the Hon. John B. Aird and the other for Gerald P. Dunn of Bala fame. These boats are all still on the Lakes.

As more speed was requested, in 1957 the 19-footer was increased to 20 ft. to accommodate a 100 H.P. engine and a few 185 H.P. V-8 engines were used in the 21-footers. Under more power the 21-footers' lap bottoms with steam bent ribs would not stand up satisfactorily, so in 1961 the design was changed to seam and batten construction with sawn frames and a hard chine. This model proved to be very successful and these boats were built until production was discontinued in '68.

Over the years, many different men came and went at Duke's, but there were some who became institutions around the Shop. Charles' brother Arthur, who had worked at the Disap-

12. Hacker designed 22', built from 1954-1956.

13 - 14. Duke Model brought out in 1940 in both 19 and 21' size. Aud Duke at controls.

pearing Propeller Boat Company, started in 1926 and spent the rest of his working life there. A good all-'round wood worker, he did a lot of planking as well as finishing.

Claude Duke was a qualified boatbuilder and also sold many boats around the Lakes in the summers from Muskoka Lakes to Georgian Bay, Lake of Bays, the lakes at Huntsville and Magnetawan. Claude died in 1979.

Aud Duke was in charge of the mechanical machine work and new engine installation as well as general manager.

Lionel Cope started in the early 1930s as a wood worker but over the years became very proficient in mixing stains and varnishing. The famous "piano finish" on Duke boats was a credit to his skills. For the last several years he has been doing this work exclusively.

Other men, with various abilities worked at other times. Ron Butson, a key craftsman, joined the staff in 1960 and was still there when the business was sold. To name others: Chas Amey, Stan Carr, Vern Carr, Clem Clancy, Lloyd Cope, Lloyd Croucher, Bill Dauncey, Jim Duggan, Rupert Duke, Ernest Duke, Ian Duke, Barry Duke, Gordon Fairhall, Cecil Fraser, Vernon Harris, Darrel McFadyen, Alf Mortimer, Geo. Moyes, Robt. Newman, Bert Riddiford and Eric Stephen. Chas. Phillips was upholsterer in later year. During the war years, Sydney Penney, Mel Wallace, Ivet Stephen etc. were with Dukes. Office workers included Bruce Hanna, Mary Wallace, Reta Duke Calverley, Darcy Duke, Alva Duke Wilson and Dorothy Duke.

Wages for boat building were always a sore spot. Hammer and saw carpenters could go out and frame up the side of a house and show something for their day's work, making more money than a good boat builder. Somehow, though, there was a fascination for boat building. Most men took great pride in their work and stayed at it a lifetime.

15. 21' Vee bottom, 1965. Driven by Bert Duke's grandson John Duke, with Aud's daughter Mary Duke.

16. 21' Vee bottom, 1966, built for Allan R. Moses.

After Charlie's death in 1954, Duke Boats became incorporated, the principals being Aud H. Duke, Claude S. Duke and Alva Duke Wilson. From the late 1950s, the restoration of older boats gradually became more important than new-boat building. In 1977 Duke Boats Limited was sold to Ed Skinner and Rick Terry, who changed the name to Duke Marine Services Ltd. and have successfully continued the same type of work.

17. *Employees in 1956*
   Back row (left to right) Aud Duke, Lionel Cope, Darrel McFadyen, Clem Clancey, Arthur R. Duke.
   Front row (left to right) Alva Duke Wilson, Stan Carr, Claude Duke, Robert Farrow, George Moyes, Robert Newman.

18. *The Shop in 1961.*

THE WAR

The Second World War brought contracts for war work that employed hundreds of men throughout the district in the different works and yards. The winter of 1940 saw a flurry of orders for commercial building, but as the war effort geared up throughout the Dominion in the summer of 1940, pleasure boat building ceased entirely. Small shops such as W.J. Johnston's (Young Billy's) spent the war building Rowing Whaler boats for the Royal Canadian Navy. Bigger operations like Dukes took on contracts building 23-foot rowing tenders and later, 25-foot motor cutters powered by 25 H.P., two-cylinder diesels. All operations worked flat-out, taking on extra hands. However, the major players in the game were Greavettes, Port Carling Boat Works and Minett-Shields.

Greavettes obtained a contract to build nine Fairmiles for the Royal Canadian Navy in 1941 and in order to have access to the Great Lakes, they leased Sachau's plant in Toronto, hiring Hans Sachau as Superintendent. The plant had to be enlarged considerably and as many parts as possible were made at Greavettes in Gravenhurst. Three boats were built at the same time. Hans Sachau stayed with Greavettes until eight of the boats were built, at which time he left to go into a company making smaller wooden parts for large compasses, etc. Bill Hall was plant superintendent for the last Fairmile. According to Ron MacNab, Greavettes finished the first Fairmile so nicely the Navy authorities brought in officials from the other contracting companies to see her.

The Port Carling Boat Works had established a branch operation in Honey Harbour on Georgian Bay — first under Doug Milner and after 1935 under his brother Cam. In 1940 they, in

conjunction with Minett Shields, built a factory and took orders to build four "Fairmiles". The Fairmile was a 112-foot "B" Class motor launch designed by the Fairmile Company of the United Kingdom, hence its name. Fairmiles saw extensive service in the Gulf of the St. Lawrence and the Caribbean. In all, 59 came from the Great Lakes boatyards and of these 11 were built in Honey Harbour. At one point, four Fairmiles were set up in the factory and a crew of between 300 to 350 men were working on them. As much work as feasible was done in Port Carling and Bracebridge, from bunks to half frames, and then trucked down to Orillia and up the Coldwater Road to Honey Harbour for fabrication. After the first four Fairmiles were constructed, the Boat Works and Minett-Shields parted company. Minett-Shields took on the task of building two sizeable 46-foot Harbour craft on their own and the Boat Works continued independently building seven more Fairmiles and two mine sweepers.

The Mine Sweepers were of the "Lake" Class. These were copies of the Admiralty-type 126-foot wooden-hulled mine sweeper. The R.C.N. placed orders for 16 of these boats but only 13 were started and of these just 10 were completed before V.J. day. The remaining three were finished for civilian use.

The Port Carling Boat Works were responsible for building two mine sweepers; BIRCH LAKE (Pennant No. T483) and PINE LAKE (Pennant No. T492). The BIRCH LAKE was never commissioned but was completed and sold to the Bowswater Co. of Newfoundland as the M.V. ASPY III after the war. The PINE LAKE was finished in September of 1945 and turned over to the U.S.S.R. as T195. A crew of 32 Russians, including the famous Russian spy Igor Gouzenko, spent three months in Honey Harbour watching the PINE LAKE's fitting-out.

The aftermath of the story in the post-war period was not as happy for Port Carling Boat Works. The Dominion Government — ever so conscious of the feeling after the First War of wartime profiteering — reopened the contracts and imposed a cost-plus ceiling on the World War II contracts that had been let. The Port Carling Boat Works had not set up operations in that way and had built a cushion into its pricing to allow for unforeseen contingencies. The government determined that the Boat Works owed it $140,000. This would have forced the company into bankruptcy but after several months of negotiation a lesser figure was settled on.

1. *Fairmiles at Honey Harbour.*
(page 135 - 136).

2. *One of 50 27' whalers built by*
W.J. Johnston during W.W. II.

3. *A 25' motor cutter built by Duke.*

4. *Rescue boats built by Greavette in*
Gravenhurst.

5. *The minesweeper PINE LAKE*
built by the Port Carling Boatworks
in Honey Harbour.

EARL BARNES

Earl Barnes was another of the independent builders working out of Bracebridge. A very clever mechanic and woodworker, he also made a name for himself as a boat designer.

Originally Barnes worked for Bert Minett but he struck out on his own in 1926, buying an old house on Slater Street in Bracebridge and pulling out the partitions on the ground floor to make room for two boats. Here he built one or two launches a year until he folded in 1937. Throughout these years he was helped by Doug Fraser of Bracebridge, and his wife Gladys Barnes.

In his first several years of business, Barnes' launches closely resembled Minett-Shields displacement boats. While his hardware was almost identical to his old employers' to begin with, it became increasingly individualistic through the 1920s. Barnes designed everything he built; he made all his own patterns for deck hardware, molded his own aluminum stems, and he and his wife did all their own upholstery. The end result was a very smart looking craft.

Barnes' boats bore a trademark that made them readily identifiable in the fleet. He admired the Indian head on the Pontiac cars of the day, made a model of it and mounted it on the bows of his boats.

Barnes started building hard-chine boats in 1930; he built two for Fred Burgess of Burgess Island, Lake Joseph and Toronto, and a 26-footer for Mr. Welsman on the same Island. In the winter of 1933/'34 Earl started building the very clean, streamlined boats that became his best known. A speedboat was built for T. Lang Moffat (of the Moffat Manufacturing Co.) and it was successfully raced on these lakes — and more importantly won in its class in 1936 at the

1. PEGGY, built in 1931. Earl Barnes in boat with Gladys Barnes and Mrs. Finlayson.

2. WILL-O-THE-WISP, built for Lang Moffat and now owned by Ron Lang, Arnprior.

3. BILLY BEA II, 22', 1936. Built for Dr. Charlton, now owned by Jim McKee.

C.N.E. Only 19 and one-half feet in length, it had a beam of six feet and was powered with a 6 cylinder Chrysler. Two years later in (1935/'36) he built a 22-footer for Dr. Charlton (a brother-in-law of Lang Moffat) with a torpedo stern. It was shown at the Toronto Boat show in 1936 to a very favourable public. Nevertheless Barnes went bankrupt in 1937; interest does not always translate into orders.

A number of Barnes' boats went to Peninsula Lake in the Huntsville area and some to these lakes. Over the years he built the BRANT for John Ham of Brant Island on Bala Bay, a boat for Manning Doherty whose cottage was near the Muskoka Lakes Golf and Country Club, as well as the boats for the Wellsmans and the Burgesses. While he was building one of the boats for Burgess in the early 1930s, Fred Burgess came up to Bracebridge for a spell and worked with Earl and Doug on his own boat.

According to Ron Lang, Earl Barnes consulted and designed for Shepherd Boats and was approached on several occasions to work for Chris Craft. Lang also has it on good authority that Barnes did design work for a firm in the U.S. that built racing boats. Lang suspects that firm was 'Ventnor' because of its connection with Minett-Shields.

After Barnes shut down in Bracebridge, he and two men went to Hamilton where they built one launch for a man who owned a car repair shop. Immediately prior to the war he went to the U.K. to work for the English division of Moffat, but returned with the outbreak of war to work for the government designing small craft. After the war he was occupied in converting Fairmiles and designing small craft and cruisers. Issues of Canadian Boating from the 1950s carry a number of his designs for small runabouts and outboards.

BORNEMAN

The Ditchburn operations in Gravenhurst were so large that people often forgot that there were other builders in town. Julius and Herman Borneman started a small boatworks on Gull Lake in 1909 and remained in business until 1924 when they took on the Ford agency in Gravenhurst.

Originally they were occupied exclusively with the building of canoes and rowboats, but they started building power boats before the First World War. At least two men worked for them: Abe Wishman and Sonny Hanson.

The Bornemans built launches in a way that was unique, at least to this district; they built them like a canoe. Built on a mold, their ribs were bent over the mold and planked afterward. While a great number of their boats were built of cypress, the two existent boats that we are aware of still on the lakes are both fine mahogany launches.

1. Borneman's shop on Gull Lake.

2. Typical early (c. 1914) launch.

3. LLANSAKES built in 1919 for the Irwins and now owned by Rob Purves.

4. Peter Jennings in his recently restored Borneman.

CLIVE J. BROWN

Clive Brown was an independent builder from Bracebridge whose career spanned close to 50 years. Self-taught, he started building boats before the First War in a small shop behind his family home on McMurray Street opposite the public school. A perfectionist — not a production man — he always worked alone, building boats to his own designs or from plans from New York, Detroit, or his customers.

While Brown is thought to have built a boat per year only, about two dozen of these are known to have been classic launches. His earliest known major commission was the 27-footer SQUIRREL in 1914 for W.L. Mellon of Beaumaris. Fifteen years later he was to build another 27-footer for the Mellons: the BIG BOY II, for $1,750. Incidentally, Brown sold all his boats at only 20% above cost which helps explain why he did not die a wealthy man.

Among those who commissioned boats from Brown were Carl Borntraeger of Cinderwood Island of Beaumaris; both Reuben and Harvey Miller of Beaumaris, and the Brogans of Mortimer's Point and Buffalo. This last boat, the WEST WIND, was a 24-footer built in 1922. It was typical of a style Brown favoured through the 1920s: a double-ender of cedar lapstrake construction with a varnished spruce deck. It is a very pleasing little boat with its painted black hull and slim lines. His clinker-built boats were all bolted together with brass bolts. He was also known for using four-cylinder Star engines that were converted for marine use by either himself or Norman Scholey.

In the late '50s, just before his death in 1959, he built a launch for the George Ecclestone family of Bracebridge, but his last really interesting boat was built for Nelson M. Davis of Beaumaris

and Toronto. The ROCKET is a 22-foot, stream-lined, mahogany planing launch built over two or three years in the late 1940s and powered with a V8 Interceptor engine. It has two cockpits forward with the engine mounted aft. The stern has a pronounced tumble home and a transom binder that sweeps right up over the deck. Brown's boats are not well-known today but there are still several of them on the lakes witnessing his skill and artistry.

1. WEST WIND, 24', built for the Brogans of Mortimer's Point and Buffalo in 1922 and owned today by Montegu Black.

2. ROCKET, 20' built in 1948 for Nelson Davis and powered today with a V-8 215 H.P. Intercepter. Present owner Irving Lindzon.

MCNEIL & NORRIS

McNeil Norris is one of the lesser-known builders on these lakes. Oliver Alexander McNeil and William Henry Norris were brothers-in-law who formed a partnership in 1918 in Bala for the purpose of establishing a boat livery, doing general repair work, and selling marine supplies as well as building launches. Bill Norris was the boat builder of the two. During the winter while Ollie McNeil was up north prospecting, Bill Norris and a helper built one boat per winter in their shop through the 1920s and more infrequently in the 30s, until the start of the Second World War. According to Reg Walker, their total output was approximately a dozen boats from 24 to 36-foot in length, centre-drive or forward drive, with smoothskin displacement hulls and Vee bottoms.

Boats were only built in the winter. In the summer they operated what we would call today a marina; servicing boats, selling gas and selling Peterborough Canvas Canoes (for $80.00).

In 1922 they built a 36-foot mahogany launch with cypress bottom for their own livery and freight work but she was too large for their shop, so they set her up in an old unheated barn which belonged to the Currie family. Here she was planked and the hull finished. It must have been terrifically cold and uncomfortable trying to do boat work without heat! Reg Walker remembers this launch was moved out to have the decks etc. installed and finished up. He did not know where she was moved but Matheson's grandson John Dixon believes she was finished in his grandfather's shop. McNeil Norris used her awhile then sold her to A. Bickmore of Mortimer's Point for their passenger boat at Pleasant View Hotel. It appears she is the only McNeil Norris boat around today although there may be others of which we haven't heard.

McNeill Norris had a garage and taxi business across the street from their boat shop. Reg Walker started to work for McNeil Norris before he was old enough to legally drive a car but he took a few local trips before he was of age and later made trips to Gravenhurst and all points south to Toronto. In the winters he worked with Bill Norris building boats but he was not old enough to have worked on the 36-footer PLEASANT VIEW. Reg quit in 1941 to work for Ontario Hydro.

McNeil Norris built a 26-foot Hacker-designed Vee bottom with a double skin bottom for a Toronto stock broker in 1928. She was powered with a Kermath 225 H.P. engine with overhead camshaft. One rather unusual feature was a large cockpit aft of the engine and a small one forward of the engine from where the boat was driven. She appeared to have been designed to be chauffeur driven.

McNeil Norris built the occasional boat until 1941-42 then sold their business to W. Baldock in 1945. A few years later Baldock was killed at a railroad crossing in Bala. Walter and Edna Templeton purchased the shop in 1951 which they operated for twenty-five years as a marina, then sold it to Stan Brent who still operates the business as Norstan Marine. The garage business, which was sold to Reg Ferguson, blew up a number of years ago, killing one man.

1. Oliver Alexander McNeil 1880-1957 (left) and William Henry Norris 1879-1947.

2. PLEASANT VIEW, 36', built 1922.

3. McNeil & Norris shop in Bala.

FETTHALL BOATS

On April Fools Day, 1929, David Fettis and Wilfred Hall went into partnership, forming a company to build boats on Gravenhurst Bay just back of the Ditchburn plant. Wilf had been employed by Bert Minett and Dave had been working for a pattern-maker named Scott in Toronto.

According to Evan Fraling, Wilf wanted to build a boat every bit as good as any of Bert Minett's, so he built one 28-foot displacement launch for his half-brother Herbert Hall who stayed at the Royal Muskoka Hotel each summer. As Evan remembers it, this launch was a Minett, as far as lines and construction went. Powered by an 8-cylinder Niagara Engine with a supercharger, it never proved entirely successful — the engine never did work properly. However, Fettis and Hall planned to make their reputation — and their fortune — building stock 18-foot boats. These were very stylish and attractive. Bill Ogilvie, who sold their boats in Toronto, describes them as being very light and close-ribbed; as using "airplane construction". Their first year proved successful as they used a very light (250 lb.), 25 H.P. Van Blerck Jr. engine that turned up a very high speed. The next season they installed the same engine but Van Blerck had stepped it up to 35 H.P. and it did not work out.

Dave Fettis is said to have made half a dozen trips to a customer near Kingston, often as not with a new engine, to try to keep him happy — but to no avail. The team built about 18 of these boats in two or three years but, plagued with engine difficulties, could not make a go of it.

After the failure of their business both went to work at Greavette, and Wilf Hall eventually became one of the company's key men overseeing the construction of one of their Fairmiles on the Humber River in Toronto during the last war.

AMES

Strictly speaking Ames does not fa within the scope of this work but w are including a brief note as all the work was brought to these lakes.

Albert Ames started work in a sho run by Herb Ditchburn in Trento during the last War. After workin at Hunter's in Orillia, he move back to Muskoka in the early '5C and started working for Dou Brown on Lake Joseph. Mr. Brow commissioned a series of fiv launches over the years rangin from 18 to 28 feet in length. Albe would build one each winter in h shop in Orillia.

Two of his boats are illustrated right.

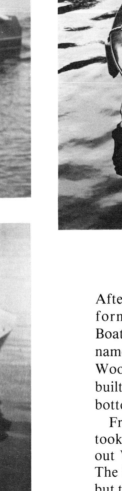

MATLO

After the Second World War, Dick Steele, a former employee of the Port Carling Boatworks, together with a Scots boatbuilder named Frank Cull, built a shop on the Woodroffe property in Footes Bay. Here they built a number of small smoothskin vee-bottom launches.

Frank Cull was the builder and eventually took over the shop and subsequently bought out Vince Robinson in Port Sandfield as well. The business didn't last more than a few years but they did build a very classy little boat.

We have illustrated here one of the few remaining on the lakes, the PETMAR, owned by Peter Foster.

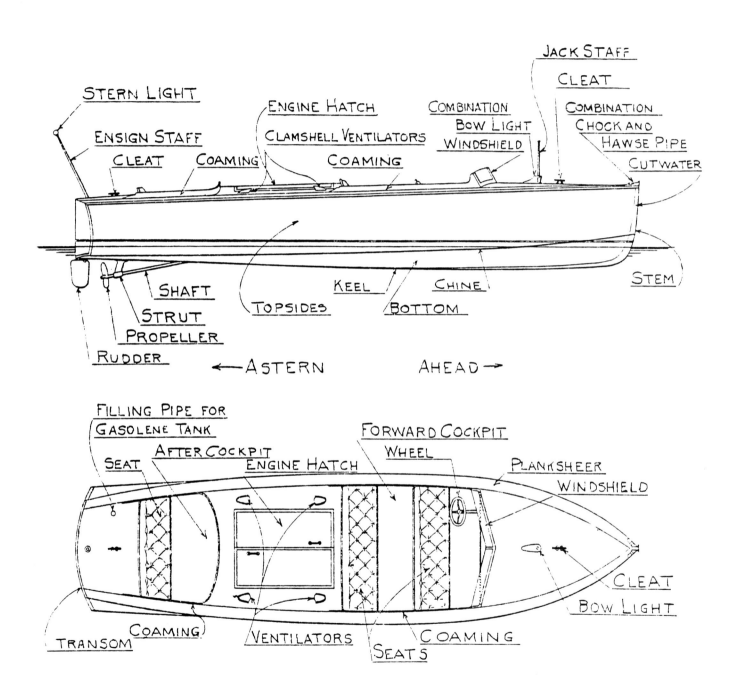

STERN LIGHT

ENSIGN STAFF

CLEAT   COAMING

ENGINE HATCH

CLAMSHELL VENTILATORS

COAMING

COMBINATION
BOW LIGHT
WINDSHIELD

JACK STAFF

CLEAT

COMBINATION
CHOCK AND
HAWSE PIPE
CUTWATER

SHAFT

STRUT

PROPELLER

RUDDER

TOPSIDES

KEEL   CHINE

BOTTOM

STEM

←ASTERN   AHEAD→

FILLING PIPE FOR
GASOLENE TANK

SEAT   AFTER COCKPIT

ENGINE HATCH

FORWARD COCKPIT

WHEEL

PLANKSHEER

WINDSHIELD

CLEAT

BOW LIGHT

TRANSOM   COAMING

VENTILATORS   COAMING

SEATS

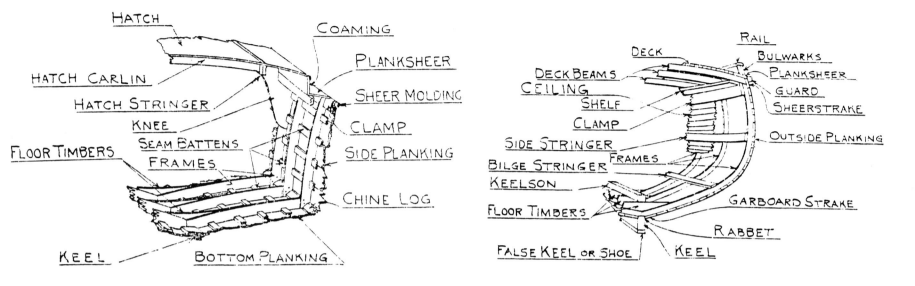

ILLUSTRATIONS

Every reasonable care has been taken to trace ownership of copyrighted material. Information will be welcome which will enable the publishers to rectify any credit in subsequent editions. Acknowledgement is made to the following sources for illustrative material used in this book; reference in each case is to the picture number. All photographic copying work was by A.H. Duke.

TITLE PAGE: Lorraine McNab. **INTRODUCTION:** 1, 4 A.H. Duke; 5 W.m. Gray. **BOAT BUILDING:** J.C. Gray. **DITCHBURN:** 2 Lorraine MacNab; 3-8, 11, 18-20 Mrs. Parker; 9 Chas. Smith; 10, 14 Gravenhurst Archives Committee; 12, 15-17, 21, 29, 36 Bruce Wilson; 13, 22, 23, 24, 28, 43 John Gray; 25, 30, 31, 34 Mrs. Hare; 26 James Woodruff; 27, 32, 33, 35, 37, 39, 40 A.H. Duke; 44 Charles McCulley. **MINETT-SHIELDS:** 1, 3, 4, 14, 15, 22 Mrs. Johnston; 2 Bill Minett, 5 Mrs. Hare, 6-9, 23, 25, 29, 31, 34, 43-45 A.H. Duke; 10, 18, 20, 30 Les Goodfellow; 13 W. P. Snyder III; 16 Dorothy Duke; 18, 19 Paul Doddington; 24, 26 James Woodruff; 27, 28, 32 Mrs. Shields; 36, 37 John Gray; 38-42 Fred Burgess. **GREAVETTE:** 1 Lorraine MacNab; 2, 3-6, 8, 9, 12-19, 21-23, 26 Bruce Wilson; 10, 20 A.H. Duke, 11, 24, 25 John Gray; 24 Port Carling Pioneer Museum. **PORT CARLING BOATWORKS:** 2-4 John Dixon; 7, 8 Paul Doddington; 9, 10 Paul Gockel; 11-18 Chas. McCulley. **JOHN MATHESON:** 2, 3, 5 John Dixon; 4 Alvin Judd; 6, 7 A.H. Duke. **ALBERT H. DUKE:** 1 A.H. Duke; 2 John Gray; 3 Martin Gardner. **DUKE BOATS:** 1, 2, 5-18 A.H. Duke; 3, 4 Michael Vaughan. **THE WAR:** 1, 5 Chas. McCulley; 2 John Dixon; 3 Dorothy Duke; 4 Bruce Wilson. **EARL BARNES:** 1, 3 Mrs. Gladys Lazarra; 2 Ron Lang. **BORNEMAN:** 1, 2 Ray Borneman; 3, 4 A.H. Duke. **CLIVE BROWN:** 1, 2 A.H. Duke. **McNEIL & NORRIS:** 1 Ernie O'Halloran; 3 Molly Bramley. **AMES:** Doug Brown. **MATLO:** A.H. Duke. Photograph of authors by James Woodruff.

ACKNOWLEDGEMENTS

We are greatly indebted to the following people who shared with us their memories and photographs of boating and boat building in Muskoka:

Albert Ames, Charles F. Amey, Raymond Borneman, Molley Bramley, Herbert Ditchburn Jr., John Dixon, Gordon Fairhall, Dave Forman, Douglas Fraser, Marion Fry and the Gravenhurst Archives, Leslie Goodfellow, John C. Gray, Roscoe Groh, Mrs. Gordon Hare, Bert Hurst, William Jocque, Mrs. Marjorie M. Johnston (see Minett), Alvin Judd, Anne Duke Judd, Ron Lang, Mrs. Lazarra, Glen Mallory, Ron and Lorraine MacNab, C.J. McCulley, Hugh MacLennan, Peter Miller, Cam Milner, Wm. Minett, Wm. Ogilvie, Clarence Shaw, Mrs. Bryson Shields, Charlie Smith, Eric Stephen, Derek Stott, Garth Tassie, Leslie Tennant, Morris Topping, Douglas Van Patten, Reg Walker, Chas. Wheaton, Bruce Wilson, Harold Wilson, James Woodruff.

Among the abovementioned we would especially like to thank Mr. Tennant and Mr. Goodfellow, Bert Minett's daughter Mrs. Johnston, and Mrs. Bryson Shields for their invaluable help on the story of Minett-Shields. Mr. Ditchburn, Mr. Bruce Wilson and Mr. and Mrs. MacNab were especially helpful with information and photographs on the stories of Ditchburn and Greavette. We are also very grateful for the help of John Dixon and Gordon Fairhall in piecing together the story of the boatbuilders of Port Carling.

A descendant of two old Muskoka families, Sutton and Duke, Audrey Harold Duke (right) was born and raised in Port Carling. In 1926, at the age of 18, he entered his father's business, Duke Motor Service, later Duke Boats. During the winter months of the mid 1930's, "Aud" went to Toronto to further his technical and business studies.

In 1939 he married Dorothy L. Smith of Toronto and they have two daughters, Anne M. Judd and Mary L. Robinson. Community interests have included service on the Port Carling School Board and the Village Council, the Muskoka District Advisory Board of the C.N.I.B. and as a Charter and Life Member of the Port Carling Lions Club. Aud's hobby of photography has enabled him to record the fine launches and varied craft of Muskoka's historic boat building industry.

William Melville Gray (left) is a Torontonian with a keen interest in Muskoka; his family has been summering in Muskoka on Lake Joseph for close to a century. The Grays bought their first motor boat in 1900 (it was not, unfortunately, built in Muskoka, but was brought up from Toronto).

Bill's grandfather remedied this situation in 1918 by purchasing one of Bert Duke's launches. This was replaced in 1931 with another Duke boat: the OSPREY II. She was built by Aud's father Charlie and was the beginning of a long connection between the Grays and Dukes.

NOTES